Allyn and Bacon
Quick Guide to the Internet
for
Sociology

Robert Thompson
Minot State University

Joseph D. Rivard
Central Michigan Univesrity

Allyn and Bacon
Boston · London · Toronto · Sydney · Tokyo · Singapore

Robert Thompson is a Professor in Sociology at Minot State University, Minot, North Dakota.

Joseph Rivard is an Associate Professor at Central Michigan University, Mt. Pleasant, Michigan.

The Authors Online

Thompson
E-mail:
thompsor@warp6.cs.misu.nodak.edu

Rivard
E-mail:
34c5ous@cmuvm.csv.cmich.edu

Contents

Part Six
Activities to Accompany Henslin's
Sociology: A Down-to-Earth Approach,
Third Edition . . . 73

Activities to Accompany Henslin's *Essentials of Sociology* . . . 94

Get Connected Now!

Load, click and cruise on the Internet with Sprint Internet Passport
(SM) for news, information, entertainment and much more. With Sprint
Internet Passport, you get full-service, direct Internet access from Sprint,
friendly customer service support on-line or by phone 24 hours a day,
seven days a week. You'll be able to easily browse around the World
Wide Web, and you'll also receive one E-mail account for communicating with family, friends and colleagues. In addition when you get connected with Sprint Internet Passport, you'll receive full access to more
than 18,000 Usenet newsgroups, local service from more than 200 U.S.
cities (more planned in 1997) and reliable service from one of the Internet's largest carriers.

Pricing for Sprint Internet Passport is $19.95 a month for unlimited
use,* or you can pay only for the hours you use at a rate of $1.50 per
hour. For your convenience, we'll bill your VISA®, MasterCard® or
American Express®.

Just double click on the Sprint icon to start your Internet experience.

Sprint Installation Instructions

DO NOT INSTALL SOFTWARE until you have read the Software
License agreement which appears on the CD.

If you currently use Netscape® Navigator as your Internet browser,
Sprint Internet Passport will automatically overwrite that software.
However, with just a little extra care and effort, Sprint Internet Passport
will nicely coexist on your system with your current software. More information and details on the exact steps necessary to preserve your current configuration can be found at http://www.sprint.com/passport, or
you can call us at 1-800-786-1400.

---

*Nation-wide 800 Access Number includes surcharge of $4.80 per hour if local service is
not available in your area.

Windows® 3.1 Users

1. Insert the *Sprint Internet Passport* installation CD into your CD-ROM drive.

2. In *Program Manager* or *File Manager,* select *File* from the menu bar, and then select Run.

3. In the *Command Line* field, type *D:\INSTALL* (where D: represents the drive letter of your CD-ROM).

4. Click *OK,* then follow the on-screen prompts to complete the software setup. When you're prompted to do so, allow setup to restart Windows®.

5. When restart is complete, double-click on the *Sprint Internet Passport Account Setup* icon in the *Sprint Internet Passport* program group.

6. Follow the on-screen prompts to set up your *Sprint Internet Passport* account.

7. When registration is completed, double-click on the *Sprint Internet Passport* icon in the *Sprint Internet Passport* program group.

8. Click *Dial.*

You're ready to begin!

Windows95® Users

1. If you have never been on-line before, be sure to have your Windows95® diskettes or *Sprint Internet Passport* CD handy.

2. Insert the *Sprint Internet Passport* installation CD into your CD-ROM drive. On most systems, the setup process will begin automatically within about 10 seconds.

3. If the setup program doesn't begin automatically, click the *Start* button on your Task Bar and then click *Run.* In the *Run* window, type

D:\INSTALL (where *D:* represents the drive letter of your CD-ROM) and click *OK.*

4. Follow the on-screen prompts to complete the software setup. If you're prompted for a Windows95® diskette, place the required diskette in *Drive A:;* if you're prompted for the Windows95® CD, remove the *Sprint Internet Passport* CD from your CD-ROM drive and insert your Windows95® CD. If you're prompted to do so, allow set up to restart your computer.

5. Double-click the *Sprint Internet Passport Account Setup* icon in the *Navigator* window.

6. Follow the on-screen prompts to set up your Sprint Internet Passport account.

7. Once registration is completed, double-click on the *Dial Sprint Internet Passport* icon on your desktop to connect to Sprint Internet Services.

8. If the password field is blank (no stars), enter your password.

9. Click Connect.

10. Double-click the *Sprint Internet Passport* icon on your desktop to launch the Sprint Internet Passport Browser (Netscape Navigator).

You're ready to begin!

Macintosh Users

1. Insert the Sprint Internet Passport installation CD into your CD-ROM drive.

2. The *Sprint Internet Passport* window will appear on your desktop. Inside this window, double-click the *Installer* icon.

3. Follow the on-screen prompts to complete the software setup. Be sure to take the default settings. (Note that default settings are outlined in black on your screen.)

4. When setup is complete, you will be prompted to restart your computer. Click on *Restart.*

5. When restart is complete, the Account Setup window appears. Click on the *Next* arrow in the Account Setup window.

6. Follow the on-screen prompts to set up your Sprint Internet Passport account.

   During Account Setup, your computer will attempt to connect to the registration service to open your account. *If you are using Macintosh System 7.1,* you will be prompted to restart your computer. Click on Restart. When restart is complete, the Account Setup window appears. Click on the *Connect Now* arrow to continue with Account Setup.

7. When registration is complete, you will be prompted to restart your computer. Click on *Restart.*

8. When restart is complete, double-click on the *Sprint Internet Passport* icon in the Sprint Internet Passport window. *FreePPP* will connect you to Sprint Internet Services, and the Sprint Internet Passport browser will launch.

You're ready to begin!

Exiting your Sprint Internet Passport Account

If you're using Windows® 3.1

- Close *Sprint Internet Passport (Netscape Navigator)* by clicking on *File* and then clicking on *Exit.*
- Close any other open Internet client applications (e.g., IRC, FTP, and Telnet sessions).
- Disconnect from *Sprint Internet Passport* by clicking the *Disconnect* button in the *Sprint Internet Dialer* box.

If you're using Windows95®

- Close *Sprint Internet Passport (Netscape Navigator)* by clicking on *File* and then clicking on *Exit.*
- A message will come up stating that there are open modem connections. Choose "yes" to disconnect from the Internet.

- Close any other open Internet client applications (e.g., IRC, FTP, and Telnet sessions).
- Check to make sure there is no button on the Task Bar labeled *Connected to Sprint Internet*. If there is, click on it to bring up the *Sprint Dialer Dialogue* box and click on the *Disconnect* button.

If you're using a Macintosh

- Close *Sprint Internet Passport (Netscape Navigator)*.
- Double-click on the FreePPP Setup icon in the Sprint Internet Passport folder.
- Click Disconnect.

Notes

Be sure to record your:

- Dial Access Number
- Sprint Internet Passport Password
- E-mail Address
- Sprint Internet Passport Log-in ID

A README file has been included on your Sprint Internet Passport CD. Windows® 3.X users can find it here: *D:\WIN.31\DISK5\README.TXT* (where D: represents your CD-ROM drive). Windows95® users can access the file by clicking on Start, Clicking on Run, typing *D:\WIN.95\DISK5\README.TXT* (where D: represents your CD-ROM drive), and clicking OK.

For Macintosh users, the *README.txt File* can be found in the Sprint Internet window on the CD.

Your software will automatically search for and attempt to identify your modem. However, if setup encounters difficulties, you may need to identify your modem manually. See the *README.txt File* for more information. Be sure to verify your pricing plan selection.

Be sure your registration address matches your credit card billing address. If your credit card company uses ZIP+4, it is important that you include the extra 4 digits.

If you live in an area where local calls can span two or more area codes, you may want to modify the 1+Area Code settings in your dialer. See the *README.txt File* for more information.

Please review all the numbers available to help ensure your modem dialer is set for a local call. If you are unsure if a number is a local call, check with your local telephone company. Please note that in some areas, a call may be considered long distance, even though it does not require dialing a "1" or "0".

Part One: What Is the Internet?

Background and History

The *Internet* is a vast global network of computers connected to each other. Although it is not uncommon for many computers to be linked in an office or school network, the Internet has become the ultimate network because of its size. The Internet is the largest collection of computers connected by high-speed telephone lines that has ever been created. Because of the number of computers online, the Internet allows an individual user to access and share vast information and communication resources.

The Internet began originally as a computer network established by the Department of Defense in the 1960s. It was considered a useful tool in establishing fast and efficient military communication. By the 1970s, many major universities and research institutions joined this communication network. They began to share information resources via this new electronic backbone. The ease and speed with which individuals were able to communicate led large numbers of additional organizations to join the network.

By the late 1980s, the popularity of the Internet exploded. Users enjoyed the opportunity to access a wide variety of computer services and information, much of which was free. The number of information resources became so large that by the early 1990s many ordinary citizens found they could benefit directly from the resources on the Internet. As there were already a large number of home computers in existence, all a person needed to do to get online was to create a link from his or her computer to the Internet. Linking a home

1

computer to the Internet can be done in a number of ways that will be described in detail shortly.

Understanding the World Wide Web

The World Wide Web is one area of the Internet that has become especially popular. The Web makes extensive use of what some would call *multimedia*. In other words, the information accessed from the Web includes not only printed matter, but pictures, graphics, and sound as well. Getting around on the Web is especially user friendly because information topics can be pursued by simply pointing and clicking on topical titles. The Web is essentially a service provider that allows users to obtain a variety of information held within the resources of any number of computers on the Internet. The important thing to remember is that as the Internet grows, so too does the Web. Both constantly expand, much like gigantic spider webs alive with activity.

Web Organization and Content

The popularity of the World Wide Web is a result of its ability to make the diverse parts of the Internet more convenient to the user. The evolution of the Web has made access to the Internet much easier to both describe and use.

The Web is organized efficiently into three essential parts:

● **Content**: The Web provides the user with a huge stockpile of information to read, view, or hear. Content within the Web is usually considered the most important of its components. After all, it is the information online that prompts most people to participate on the Internet, right? One might think of the Web as an electronic library. The Web has an ever-expanding array of topics. Some of the topics are specific while others (such as "Education") are encyclopedic in nature. Information gleaned from the Web may take the form of printed matter, pictures or illustrations, sound, music, animation, and video.

In addition to the impressive assortment of reference information, the Web has become host to a great deal of commercial advertising as well. Much as our highway system has been marked with billboards advertising a variety of goods and services, our information highway is characterized in a similar fashion. The ads take the form of *Web pages* that companies create in order to provide consumers with product literature or catalog information. Some of these ads not only inform the user of product information, but allow the consumer to use the company's Web Page to purchase products while still online. Likewise, companies have created Web pages to provide consumers with product support after purchase. For example, you might take a few minutes now to access the Allyn & Bacon Sociology page at *http://www.abacon.com/sociology/sochome.html*, where several text books are offered and links to information about the texts are given. These product-support Web pages help decrease the load carried by 1-800 product support telephone lines. Web product support pages are sometimes less time consuming to use than telephone services plagued with voice recorded options and while-you-wait elevator music.

● **Client Software**: Your computer needs software in order to get all the information that is available on the Web. A *Web client* is a software program that lets you browse the content within the Web. Popular Web clients are *Mosaic,* *Netscape,* and Microsoft's *Internet Explorer.*

Much more will be said about these programs in Part Two of this Guide.

● **Servers**: The old adage that says no man is an island, applies to a computer on the Internet. In order to get all the "good stuff" on the Internet, you need to have access to other computers online. Servers are computers you can go to in order to get the information for your client software. An Internet server makes information available to online users. In order to provide the information to anyone who may request it, all the computers need to speak and understand the same *protocols*. In other words, they need to communicate in the same language. The business of computer protocols has become a bit sticky these days. There are so many different protocols it is difficult to keep track of them all. As a user, it really isn't necessary for you to understand all the technical stuff that accompanies computer protocols. However, there are a few basic vocabulary terms that you might find useful as you begin your journey on the information highway.

Tech Talk

Here is your first Internet word bank!

☐ **Browser**: Software used for exploring the World Wide Web.

☐ **HTML** (Hypertext Markup Language): Because of the diverse types of computers and computer software programs in use on the Internet, there is a need to standardize language protocols. HTML is the standardized language used on the Internet.

☐ **Hypertext and HTTP** (Hypertext Transport Protocol): Hypertext is a type of document that allows convenient links to other documents. It is a simple way of cross-referencing certain words, phrases, or symbols with additional information. Words or symbols that appear in color may be identified as *hypertext*. By clicking your mouse on these color coded words or symbols (*links*) you

4

are immediately connected to documents related to that field. The link may take you to another spot within a specific document, or to another site on the Web that contains related material to your source. HTTP is the protocol used for transferring hypertext documents on the Web. If you accessed the Allyn & Bacon Sociology page earlier, *http://www.abacon.com/sociology/sochome.html*, you experienced hypertext first hand.

- ❏ **Internet Explorer**: Microsoft's software system that acts as a browser for the World Wide Web.
- ❏ **Mosaic**: A software system that acts as a browser for the World Wide Web.
- ❏ **Netiquette**: The use of appropriate communication on the Internet.
- ❏ **Netscape**: A software system that acts as a browser for the World Wide Web.
- ❏ **Spiders**: Software programs that roam the Web collecting information for indexes.
- ❏ **Winsock**: A standard that Microsoft Windows programs use to interact with the Internet.
- ❏ **URL** *(Uniform Resource Locator):* High tech talk for a specific Internet address.

Part Two: Getting Started on the Internet

In order to get online, you will obviously need a computer. We recommend a computer with at least 16 mb RAM, although 8 mb, or even 4 mb can do the job. The more RAM you have, the easier and faster you can work with and process information being retrieved from the Internet. It doesn't matter whether you are using a Macintosh or PC Windows system, as long as a modem is connected to your computer. Some computers have built in modems; others do not. If you do not have a built in modem, you will need to purchase one.

Modem is short for *mod*ulate/*dem*odulate. This is the device that allows your computer to speak to other computers via a telephone line. The modem will dial up the required access number and put you online.

If you must purchase a modem, keep in mind that not all modems are created equal. Some move data more quickly than others. The faster your modem, the faster you can send and receive data and the less time your computer spends on the telephone line. Modem speed is described in *bps* (bits per second), sometimes referred to as *baud.* While older modems transmitted at 1200 baud, those now available can operate at speeds well beyond 9600.

Once you have your modem and have properly connected it to your computer, be certain to plug the phone line into the modem before dialing up!

Service Providers

In order to begin your journey on the Internet, you will first have to establish an *Internet Account*. This can be done in several ways. If you are a university student, you should be able to establish an account through the university computer services department. Your link to the Internet will probably be routed through the university mainframe, or some form of direct connection. The good news here is that your account may be free! The bad news is that an overloaded mainframe on your campus may result in your not being able to log on whenever you want to. Daytime and evening hours may be flooded with mainframe users, and you might not always be able to gain access.

Individuals who do not have access to free university accounts may choose either an *ISP* (Internet Service Provider) or a *CSP* (Commercial Service Provider).

ISPs: There are a number of Internet Service Providers that are reasonable in cost.

There are several questions you should ask before you sign up with any service provider:

- What kinds of accounts does it offer? Some dial up services provide only Internet E-mail services. While this is great for electronic correspondence and social chit-chat, it is only one restrictive use for the Internet.
- What will your account cost per month?
- How much online time do you get for a given fee?
- What specific services will be provided? Many ISPs are dial-up bulletin board services, and may restrict the type of information you have access to.

- How difficult is it to get access to the service provider? Be careful of "bargain basement" dial-ups, because they may have more accounts than they can easily handle. If you are a night owl and don't mind dialing up at 2:00 a.m., this might not be a problem. However, if you need consistent and spontaneous access to the Internet, question your ISP before writing a check. Ask them about the number of accounts they have in comparison to the number of telephone lines they control.
- Do they have a customer support line?
- Will you need to install special software for your computer?

CSPs*:* Commercial Service Providers are an excellent way to gain access to the Internet if you can afford the monthly premiums. CSPs offer a large number of access plans and do not restrict privileges to one type of information service.

❏ **America Online** (http://www.aol.com/): America Online was established in 1989 and has become a big hit with the general citizenry of our fair land. At the time of this writing, it is hailed as the largest online service, but there are many contenders for that crown. Part of what has contributed to AOL's popularity is the neat and clean interface that has been developed for the consumer. Upon subscribing, members are shipped a very user friendly *GUI* (Graphical User Interface, software to load onto your computer that will help you surf the Net). The GUI is visually appealing and has numerous clickable buttons that give the user easy access to a host of consumer services that America Online can provide for their customers.

America Online Services

- E-mail capability
- file transfer
- gopher interface
- mail lists
- message boards
- news groups
- online magazines
- online tutorials

Although America Online offers users several plans, it is unique in that it supports a single fee structure. In other words, you pay a flat rate and have access to all AOL services.

❏ **Compuserve** (http://www.compuserve.com): The Compuserve *Information Service* (CIS) dates back to 1979 and was the first online Internet service. At that time CIS primarily served business interests as a text-only information source.

Compuserve was the first service to provide consumers with international access. It pioneered intercontinental E-mail service, so it made little difference whether users were logging on from Michigan or the Middle East.

CIS provides its subscribers with a GUI that is flexible but sometimes puzzling to the beginner. It features a *BOW* ("bunches of windows") interface that will enable the experienced user to open innumerable windows for navigating and exploring. For novices, it can be pretty scary, and they may soon be lost in the maze of windows.

Other consumer criticisms of the CIS system have to do with member addresses. Most online services allow you to select your own access name. Compuserve will assign you an account number as an ID source. This may be efficient, but it can make the ID hard to remember, and remove some of the fun and personality of online identity.

News groups on CIS have traditionally focused on news and financial information. User demand has broadened the news group focus, however, and Compuserve now features an interesting array of educational materials. The "Education Forum" has been an especially popular Compuserve feature. This service allows educators to do online projects together, download vast amounts of educational freeware and shareware materials, or simply exchange ideas and opinions on diverse topics related to the field of education.

Although Compuserve does have a lot to offer the subscriber, much of what is available is tricky to find. The bunches of windows make topical finds elusive. The novice is better off employing a "seek and find" technique by using *Go* commands or *Search* features. A nifty plus is the free subscriber magazine that will inform you of new service options and helpful tips for CIS users.

Compuserve has a fee structure much different from that of America Online. Similar to the fee structure of premium channels on cable TV, subscribers pay a low monthly premium but must pay additional charges in order to get some of the really good materials. Be wary if you are surfing and wander into the realm of a Plus service! Compuserve's vigilant billing computers kick in, and you could be surprised at how quickly your monthly charges will escalate. If you are not able to resist spontaneous temptations, you're better off asking Compuserve for special navigator software, which requires you to identify the areas of the Internet you want to explore before logging on.

❐ **Prodigy** (http://www.prodigy.com): A relative newcomer to the field, Prodigy was conceived in 1990. IBM and Sears were the proud parents of this new cyber child, and Mom and Dad hoped their child might help other children. It would be an online service with a family focus! Prodigy features a multitude of topics, games, and news groups that are specially designed for families. Educational content is in high demand, and Prodigy even provides a special Classroom Prodigy service that is commercial free.

Prodigy is especially easy to navigate, featuring large buttons to click on that lead subscribers to various screens with lots of options. Prodigy separates the "home, family, and kids" features from the "education" features by creating two separate button fields. The reference and educational sources that are provided are immense.

Originally Prodigy was designed only for PCS. It has since expanded to include Macs, as well as specific integration with Microsoft Windows and Netscape. It has recently contracted with Microsoft to provide a version compliant with Windows95 and Internet Explorer.

Prodigy has a fee structure similar to Compuserve's in that Prodigy charges extra for its "Premium" services.

❏ **Delphi** (http://www.delphi.com): Getting online with Delphi is easy, since subscribers don't need any extravagant software to load on start up. Just dial up and you're on your way. The service offers complete Internet access but is not especially attractive. The interface is text-only, although it is fairly easy to navigate if you can remember all the control commands! One feature that is appealing to some consumers is the large number of online shopping connections.

When this was written, Delphi offered an *Unlimited Access Plan* for a monthly fee of $23.95.

❑ **GEnie** (http://www.genie.com) GEnie is noted for it's multiple player games. The graphics developed by this service provider are tremendous! If you are looking for this type of entertainment, GEnie is for you. In addition to games, GEnie also provides news groups that have been divided into twenty-one categories. The "directory of roundtables" is what GEnie likes to call the discussion menu. While there is a lot here, it can be difficult to find. It may be worth the effort however, because GEnie does not charge extra for access to the categories within the Roundtables.

Evaluating the Best Service Provider

Before you subscribe to any provider, consider carefully what services you really want. Below are listed many of the more frequently used categories offered by Internet service providers. Which of these most appeal to you? Check those that have a *high priority for you*. By reviewing your needs and interests, choosing an Internet service provider becomes a bit easier.

Which services do *you* consider a priority?

__Downloading files	__Live chit-chat
__Easy interface	__Magazines
__Educational topics	__Message boards
__E-mail	__Newspapers
__Encyclopedia	__News groups
__Financial info	__Research
__Games	__Shopping Sports
__Help online	__Weather
__Internet access	__Web access
__Kids stuff	

Keep in mind that university mainframes, university direct-connection services, and service providers such as Compuserve or America Online can only give you *access* to the Internet. In and of themselves they are not the Internet. If you think of the Internet as a great highway, you can think of service providers as gateways or on ramps. Each service provider removes many of the difficulties you would face trying to go online without one.

Service providers make using areas of the Internet easier through selective use of assorted software programs. Because the World Wide Web has become an extremely popular part of the Internet, developing Web client software has become big business. Prodigy has developed its own Web client. Other gateways use one of several best-selling web clients. Two popular Web clients are described below. Regardless of your Net connection, if you navigate the Web you will likely end up utilizing one of the packages described here.

Web Client Software

❐ **Netscape**: Netscape has become the premier Web browser to date. One reason for its success is its visual and aesthetic appeal. The graphics on Netscape are well done and the graphic capabilities for those who want to create Web pages are very versatile, allowing the user to manipulate not only text, but a mixture of textual and graphic information as well.

Netscape Basics: Information presented on Netscape appears in *hypertext*. A hypertext document allows many related topical themes to be connected by establishing *links*. Two frequently used terms in the world of hypertext are *link* and *node*. Links are connections between the conceptual elements of a project, and nodes contain text, images, or other related information within the information base. A link is essentially a navigation pathway, while a node incorporates any of the content elements, including text, images, sound bytes, and documents. For the relationship between links and nodes to be effective, it must be logical and make sense to users. In Netscape, links appear as underlined text. (In describing the features, we are using Netscape Navigator 3.0 as the model. Other versions will have a somewhat different look.) Using your computer mouse, place the pointer over any underlined text and click. Immediately you will be taken to a different document on the Web.

Netscape always allows you to see the Web address (URL) you are currently viewing by looking in the text space to the right of *Netsite* (near the top of the Netscape window). If you click on a link and decide the document isn't worth the journey, simply click on the *Back* icon in the tool bar or open the *Go* menu and select *Back*. While this sounds simple enough, if you are a new user and wander long and far enough, you may get a little lost. Fortunately, Netscape provides an easy way for you to return *home* (to the very first page you started on) by clicking on the *Home* icon on the toolbar or clicking *Home* under the *Go* menu.

Since the Web can connect you to any number of databases, you should realize that some documents will be much larger than others. The longer the document, the more time it will take for the file you've clicked on to appear. As you may recall from our earlier discussions, the speed with which the document appears can also be a reflection of the baud rate of the modem you're using or how many users are online. If you selected a file that seems to be taking forever to download, Netscape allows you to cancel the selection by clicking the *Stop* icon on the toolbar.

Sometimes you may have a Web address that you found in a newspaper or magazine article. In order to get to the address you must tell Netscape where you want to go. To do this, click on the *Open* button at the top of the page, then type the URL in the text box.

Please note! Typing in a URL must be done very carefully. Most Web addresses are long and tedious to type, and it is easy to mistype an address. Some are even *case specific*, so be sure to note any capitalization in the URL. Once you are sure the address you have entered is correct, click the *Open* button and Netscape will attempt to find the document.

Finally, you should realize you can print or save files discovered on the Web. To print the current Web page (not just the current screen), choose *File* from the upper left-hand corner of the screen and click on *Print*.

You can also save files to your own computer system (hard drive or disk drive), allowing you to take documents with you for use in another location without requiring access to the Web. To save a file, go to the File menu and select *Save As*. You will be greeted with a pop-up box allowing you to designate the file's name and where you want to save it.

❐ **Internet Explorer:** As we write a new edition of this guide, Microsoft is launching a challenge to Netscape for the Web server market, even distributing free software with Windows95. While there are new twists in Internet Explorer, its "feel" is enough like Netscape to allow us to bypass a detailed description.

❒ **Mosaic**: Prior to the arrival of Netscape, Mosaic was the Web browser preferred over and above other clients. Mosaic was on the scene earlier than Netscape and pioneered the appealing graphical characteristics we have come to know and admire when navigating the Web. If you are unable to have Netscape or Internet Explorer at your command, Mosaic is the next best thing.

Mosaic Basics: Mosaic allows the navigator to accomplish the same fundamental operations described for Netscape. The user will need to take a little time to discern the subtle differences in the way Mosaic's toolbar is laid out, however. Netscape users might criticize Mosaic's toolbar as less intuitive and thus less user friendly. There is a bank of tiny icons designed to do all the right things if you can figure out what all the symbols on the icons really mean. For example, the icon depicting an open folder launches the dialog box for entering a URL. The floppy disc icon is supposed to suggest a save-to-disc feature, while arrow keys imply forward and backward movement through document addresses. The home key is adequately characterized as a little house, and the print key aptly features a printer icon, but good luck interpreting the code for Mosaic's find, paste, and copy clipboard icons!

If you become irritated with the Mosaic toolbar you can always eliminate it all together by hiding it (open the *Options* menu and click on *Show Toolbar*). Once you remove the toolbar you might more successfully navigate through the use of conventional menus placed at the top of the computer screen.

Navigating Naturally

Whether you are a Macintosh or PC Windows user, you should be aware of several things when subscribing to an Internet provider, navigating the Internet, or browsing the Web.

❏ Internet providers will usually provide you with all the right software tools upon establishing an account but you will need to indicate when you establish your account whether you are a Mac or a PC Windows user. Net tools that are provided for either platform typically include:

- *E-mail* (send and receive electronic mail)
- *Gopher* (locate information on the Internet)
- *Veronica* (a search tool)
- *FTP* (retrieve files on the Net)
- *Archie* (a locating tool)
- *IRC* (a tool that allows "live chat" in the Net)
- *Usenet* (a "search and read" tool to access discussion topics)
- *Web client* (software to explore the Web)
- *Telnet* (a terminal on remote computers)

❏ Not all commercial service providers have Web access, and those that do may have constraints on their use. For example, some Web browsers work great for PC Windows, while Mac users are left out.

❏ GEnie's front end GUIs are only now being developed for Mac and Windows95.

❏ The *Save As* option in Mosaic works simply for Mac users. PC Window users were originally unable to have the opportunity to save a file as straight text or in HTML format. This has been rectified in current versions.

Part Three: What the Internet Can Do for You

The reasons for going online are as diverse as the people who log on. Business organizations and research institutions avail themselves of the tremendous communication and information resources that the Internet provides. Many families appreciate not only the information resources but the entertainment and online shopping features as well. Students enjoy abstract materials, the unending access to reference databases, as well as the opportunity to communicate socially and academically across the miles. Below are listed a few of the most typical kinds of services available on the Internet.

❑ **E-mail:** Electronic mail allows you to have an address on the information highway. In an instant, you can send or receive messages to any number of the 30 million plus Internet users around the globe. E-mail can be sent or received regardless of the Internet service provider to which you are connected. A Compuserve user can easily communicate with a university mainframe user, a direct connect user, a BBS user, or an America Online user.

❑**Newsgroups**: Newsgroups are essentially message boards. People read messages related to a myriad of subjects and are able to post messages about other people's messages on the Internet. It's kind of an international public forum, a large scale, electronic town meeting. Everyone can have a say on any given topic and receive feedback on individual thoughts, opinions, and suggestions.

❑ **Usenet**: Usenet consists of a large collection of newsgroups. Some are academic and scholarly, others may be amusing and fun, still others may be adult-oriented and sexually explicit. Users should keep in mind that the Internet is not monitored or policed. Since the most recent federal attempt to make explicit sex and violence on the Net illegal was struck down by the courts, language and content expressed in some newsgroups may be considered offensive by some individuals.

❑ **Mailing Lists**: These lists are essentially the same as any newsgroup, but messages are sent directly to your e-mail address.

❑ **Web Sites:** Visiting the Web gives users a break from text-only Net surfing. You can experience refreshing multimedia-based information gleaned from various Web sites containing pictures, graphics, animation, sound, or video information.

❑ **BBS:** Accessing a Bulletin Board Service entitles you to any or all of the information posted on the select BBS theme, which is generally established by the *Sysop* (systems operator). A Sysop might be a university professor or a teen-aged hacker with a passion for mountain bikes. One element that has made the BBS service so alluring is the notion of *live chat*. Live chat is a form of e-mail in which the participants simultaneously exchange text based conversation, person-to-person. Live chat lines might be established for academic, entertainment, or social purposes.

Internet Precautions

Keep in mind that, in the world of cyberspace, users have a great deal of anonymity. Many find great security in the fact that they are able to communicate with a host of individuals without ever having to provide them with personal information. Most Netters are identified with quirky code names or ID numbers.

While such anonymity can work for you, there are risks that every Netter needs to be aware of. Once online, it is difficult to know exactly with whom you are communicating. People can take on any number of false identities, or pretend to be any number of personalities. Much of this is done in a harmless social context, but some may have a criminal intent. The bottom line is simply this:

Be wary of divulging personal information.

➪ Never release your first and last name.
➪ Never divulge your resident address.
➪ Never publish your home phone number.
➪ Never reveal where you work or study.
➪ Never reveal account passwords.
➪ Never forward a picture of yourself.

Realize that many commercial service providers will ask you to fill in a *member profile* upon subscribing. There is nothing wrong with listing the type of hardware you use and your interests and hobbies, but be careful to avoid supplying personal data. Some individuals even prefer keeping their genders anonymous. This is easily done by selecting a code word that suggests neither gender.

Regardless of your precautions, individuals can still become targets of unwanted Internet communications. These communications may be intimidating, threatening, or offensive to the receiver in any number of ways. Early in your Internet experience be certain to learn how to *log* your online chat, e-mail, or messages. By compiling an accurate log of these exchanges you will be able to document experiences of intimidating or threatening messages to your Internet service provider, who will then be better able to track down and purge the offender from the system.

Finally, keep in mind that all E-mail can be *permanently* stored by a service provider. This is true *even if you delete the messages!* Beware of what you say online, especially in corporate environments wherein all E-mail becomes property of the institution. E-mail has been frequently used as evidence in court cases.

Netiquette

What is proper and what is improper communication on the Internet? A part of this issue lends itself to discussion of freedom of speech and expression, as well as academic and intellectual freedom. Few have endorsed the notion of censoring the Internet, simply because trying to discern what is universally offensive seems to be impossible. Some pictures or photos might be considered entertaining or artistic by some and pornographic by others. Assorted words are considered obscene by some, crude by others, and unexceptional by still others.

At present, the boundaries for these types of issues are relatively undefined. Some commercial service providers have begun monitoring the sending and receiving of assorted picture files. Materials deemed pornographic in nature have resulted in the procurement of criminal charges against various senders/receivers. Likewise, many CSPs will remove you from the system if, in your communication, you are prone to using inappropriate language. CSP violations typically consist of a thirty-day suspension for what is considered a violation of service terms. The extent to which these penalties increase or decrease are likely to reflect both consumer expectation and political action.

Netiquette considers far less serious and foreboding issues as well. Remaining attentive to some of the following rules will help you surf the Net without getting your feelings hurt.

■Don't take off on tangents. Experienced netters really get upset if you join a discussion group without taking the time to get acquainted with the topic and the issues. Tangents are a big pet peeve, so try to stay focused and communicate with both a point and a purpose.

■Never type in ALL CAPS. Netters interpret this as being yelled at!

■Learn a few simple Netiquette symbols such as the following:

Some examples of Netiquette symbols			
:-)	= a smile	<vbg>=	very big grin
;-)	= a wink	:-*	= kiss
:-(	= sadness	%-)	= confused
:-D	= laughter	:-|	= boring
<g>	= grin		

■Learn Netiquette shorthand. There are a number of ways to reduce the number of keystrokes necessary in order to send a message.

Some Netiquette shorthand strokes	
AND=any day now	Chris(((Chris)))=lots of hugs
B4N=bye for now	IC=I see
BBL=be back latter	ILY= I love you
BTW= by the way	IMO= in my opinion
CU= see you	J/K=just kidding
(Chris)=hug to	OIC=Oh, I see

■Flame broiled or fried? Just about the time you are really starting to enjoy surfing the net, chatting online, sending and receiving e-mail, you will probably get *flamed*. Getting flamed is a Netter's term used by some in reference to receiving rude, nasty, or meticulously critical communications. There are those on the Net who especially enjoy flaming newcomers online. These individuals will go to great lengths to insult you because of your inexperience online or your lack of Net vernacular.

There are additional situations that may set you up for getting flamed. You might be responding to a bulletin board message or sharing in an online debate or discussion group. Inevitably there will be someone who disagrees with your opinion. Instead of trying to argue a point with intellectual reasoning, some individuals will try to intimidate you with scathing criticisms about your character or writing style.

Of course there are the subtle, sneaky, humorous flames that may occasionally pop into your e-mail slot as well. These flames start out cordially, even down right friendly! Gradually the communique begins to weave in arrogant and critical commentary against you. By the time you are finished reading the note, there is little doubt in your mind that you've been had. The fiery reach of the Internet flamer knows few limits. Keep in mind that there is a difference between getting flamed and being harassed or threatened. Personal threats or harassments should be logged and reported to your Internet Service Provider.

For some, flaming has become a game. Such people consider it a part of the Net entertainment venue. Others become upset by the hostility present in such correspondence. For you budding flamers, we encourage you to fine-tune your flaming skills on Internet newsgroups dedicated to such verbal battery. For example, Usenet features a "Hall of Flame" (alt.flame.hall-of-flame). By localizing your attacks to other like-minded people, you'll allow the rest of the Internet population a well-deserved sigh of relief.

Part Four: The Impact of Media Technologies on Society

Part Three of this Guide discussed reasons for going online. Before becoming immersed in the current world of cyberspace, it seems appropriate to give consideration not only to what technology can do *for us*, but also to what it has done *to us*. What has been the impact of technology upon humankind and societies? How has it impacted daily living, and what are the questions and concerns researchers have posed within a world of advancing technological mediums? Certainly an exhaustive study exploring technology's impact on humanity is beyond the means of this Guide. What follows is a brief review of some research that has import for these issues.

This Guide has addressed itself to the Internet and the essential computing technologies that accompany its use. If we are to consider technology in its broader context, however, it is wise to remind ourselves that technology is a generic term, going far beyond the emerging technologies represented in computer-based tools. In considering the overall impact of technology upon societies, we must include the technologies which have preceded the computer age.

In order to grasp an understanding of the potential impact of computer technology, we will briefly explore the rather large body of research on assorted precomputer media technologies. The research in this area has served as a precursor to research on multi-media and interactive computing technologies.

Media and Communication

Media is the plural form of the word *medium*, and makes reference to a technology that carries information between a source and a receiver by utilizing a variety of media to convey specific messages for various purposes.

■*Media technologies* refer to a number of basic technologies involving mass or distance communication.

■*Motion media* include video, film, and television.

■*Communication* is the exchange of thoughts, messages, or information.

■*Interactive communication* requires that the exchange include reciprocal transfer of data from any number of senders and receivers.

Exploring the meaningful interpretation and comprehension of communicated information in media technologies has been an ongoing affair in contemporary societies. Internet technologies are only the latest vehicle to support our ongoing infatuation with media technology as a means of communication. Marketing specialists conjure slick, media-based advertising campaigns to sell products. Politicians use media technologies to gain political power and influence. Educators use them to facilitate instruction. Entertainment industries have captured a huge economic market through their effective use as a source of leisurely amusement and pleasure.

Even a brief excursion into media technologies raises several questions.

■ What is their research history?

■What have been the questions and concerns of a society confronted with the ever-expanding presence of media technologies?

■Are our questions and concerns about the

expansion of media technologies in society today similar to our concerns about past technologies?

Research Histories

How far back do we go when establishing a research history for media-based communication? The telegraph? The telephone? The radio? Certainly each of these had a profound impact on the way societies communicated. The advent of each revolutionized the way people exchanged information. However, our discussion will not start with any of these. Instead we will begin with the advent of motion media and the research accompanying it. Motion media technologies have had both profound societal impact and the benefit of accompanying research and study. Many studies attempted to measure the impact that motion media was having on family and community life.

The discussion of motion media technologies is especially relevant to this Guide. Motion media has become intimate with computer based technologies in a union that has conceived exciting new multimedia technologies. This makes the research review meaningful and revealing.

Research Histories to 1960

Research Snapshot

❑ **Hilde T. Himmelweit**. The earliest and most notable study in motion media research was undertaken by Hilde T. Himmelweit. As early as 1954, concerns arose over potentially adverse effects of electronic technologies. The earliest and most potent concerns regarded potentially negative effects on children and were focused on the medium of television. How would television impact the lives and learning of developing children? Television was distrusted by teachers and parents from its inception!

The Himmelweit study was initiated in England, in 1958. Few ever suspected that this would become the seminal study to which researchers would refer for decades. The study was planned by the Audience Research Department of the BBC, and attempted to discover what effect(s) this new technology was having upon children. The study became of immediate interest to American educators and parents, as television was reproducing itself rapidly in American schools and households.

One of the primary weaknesses of Himmelweit's study was the extreme broadness of its scope. It may also be criticized for its research design and the BBCs motivation in initiating such research in the first place. With widely spread rumors about this new technological marvel's negative impact on children, the BBC hoped the research would provide the public with an astute rebuttal. Himmelweit's academic credentials and her established position as a clinical psychologist and university lecturer was purported to allow the BBC a scholar's edge. At the same time, Himmelweit was encumbered by the multitude of ill-established perceptions that the BBC wanted the study to confront. One must appreciate the researcher's dilemma: to provide the academic community with a legitimate piece of scholarly investigation while placating the BBC which would fund her research.

The Himmelweit study took four years to complete and broadly explored two areas: the effects of program content upon young viewers and what was dubbed "displacement effects."

Displacement effects investigate the amount of time subjects invest in television viewing, at the expense of engaging in other activities. Subordinate to gauging the amount of viewing time invested in the medium is a consideration of the consequences of such time investments. What becomes displaced by attending to technologic media? Interpersonal relations, familial communication, play behavior, reading, homework? The study of displacement effects continues today, especially in relation to the amount of time children spend watching television, going online with computers, or playing games using recreational technology such as Nintendo.

As noted earlier, the Himmelweit study also investigated the effects of program content on children, including consideration of the medium's influence on general knowledge and academic performance in school. Of additional interest were such sociological issues as the impact of program content on social attitudes and personal values.

By now you can appreciate the host of issues and inquiries addressed by the study, which embraced a vast number of topics. We may certainly question the manner in which the study was designed and the methodology employed in tackling such a myriad of questions. Although the conclusions garnished from the Himmelweit study may be flawed, incomplete, and inconclusive, it was a significant undertaking. The study delineated a number of inquiries and issues in research related to media-based technology. It also created a working vocabulary dedicated to this type of research. Various terms coined remain a part of the lexicon used in successive investigations. Furthermore, this study inspired other studies. In this regard, the study fulfilled the expectations demanded of all good research, namely, the research was heuristic. Each succeeding study building upon the Himmelweit study became more constrained and focused.

Contents of the study: Two groups of children were studied by Himmelweit in 1958. At that time it was still possible to extract a control group composed of children unexposed to television (imagine that), as well as a group composed of television viewers. Viewers and non-viewers were matched by age, sex, IQ, background, demographics, and school grade. Thus each participant had a "twin" with whom he or she was compared. Subjects were selected from the four cities of London, Portsmouth, Sunderland, and Bristol. Approximately 4,500 children were screened to establish a studied population of 1,854 matched pairs. The sample included children in two age groups, those ages ten and eleven and those thirteen and fourteen. All children were chosen from public school systems. Data-gathering methods employed in various aspects of the study included diaries, questionnaires, personality profiles, and journals.

Summary of findings: The amount of time children invested in viewing television seemed to be influenced by five factors: habit, intelligence, personality, parental example, and the extent to which a child was predisposed to physical activity.

■When isolating intelligence as a factor involved in viewing time, intelligence was found to be positively correlated to viewing time; that is, the higher the child's intelligence, the more time watching television he or she was likely to spend.

■As a medium, television seemed to neither help nor hinder the general academic performance in middle level school children. The amount of information "transfer" from TV to school appeared negligible.

■Television had an impact on the average student's leisure-time reading habits but did not affect above- or below-average students. The study predicted that, as the novelty of television waned, the reading habits of those affected would be restored. It also suggested that television might actually complement leisure-time reading activities if/when the medium embraced elements of literary style in its televised dramas.

■The appeal of this new technological medium was enhanced by several factors. First, television was easily accessed and availability. Further, subjects felt current and up to date by having television in their homes. The appeal was also embellished by the offer of excitement and change to evening routines. In fact, television provided entertainment as an escape from such routines. Finally, it featured personalities who were inviting to watch.

■Program content was likely to affect personal values only in the presence of several other variables:
- The content must be presented in dramatic form.
- The child must be developmentally mature enough to comprehend the messages conveyed.
- The child must be emotionally sensitized to pick up subtle media cues.

■ The attention of many of the children to television was very limited and selective as a result of their varied interests and viewpoints.

■ The children were predisposed to believe many viewpoints offered them; they seem to place great faith in the "authority" of the medium.

■ Children displayed reactions to "boomerang and sleeper" effects as a result of their television viewing. These effects suggested that children may have interpreted information in less complete and less comprehensive ways than adults did. As a result, there may have been inaccuracies in the comprehension of messages conveyed by program content marketed for adult audiences.

■ Children were found to be mentally active while watching television, dispelling the presumption that since the activity is physically passive it is also cognitively passive.

The Himmelweit study was a significant research document for its time, clearly delineating the issues related to motion media technology in the 1950's. It serves as an appropriate introduction to successive studies probing the same area.

Research Histories: 1960-1970

Motion media research in the decade of the 1960s marked a continued effort to investigate those interests stimulated in the 1950s. Some interests became emotionally charged with social conscience, and other avenues of interest remained succinctly academic. In addition to researching the displacement effects of television, close examination was given to the evaluation of media content in film and television. Both the academic and emotional impact of media content upon the developing child was considered.

The impact of media-based presentation would pose hundreds of questions for both social scientists and educational psychologists, for parents and for teachers. Media-based presentation was multi-functional, and often included the presentation of information as a function of entertainment and instruction. The realization that this technology could influence knowledge, values, beliefs, and behaviors seemed overwhelming. Such realizations created a *bilateral approach to media-based research*. Such an approach is easily discriminated. There are those inquiries that are sociological and those issues that are educational.

We have noted several key questions and concerns brought forth by contributing researchers of the 1960s, noting those that are sociological and omitting those that have educational import. This decade remained a period rich in curiosity, but there was little structured research that provided specific answers to or explanations for the inquiries raised. Perhaps this was because it became increasingly clear that media-based research was much more complex than first anticipated.

Media Inquiry: Family and Society
- What is the potential impact of program content as it relates to children's behavior, personal values, and the emotional maturity of children?
- What is the impact of media technologies upon family life, familial sharing and communication, and leisure time?
- To what extent do media technologies deprive children of social interaction?
- To what extent does motion media accommodate socio-emotional needs? To what extent do media technologies encourage children to become socially isolated or escapist?
- What may be the overall cumulative effect of motion media upon children over decades?

Research Histories: 1970-1980

The advent of the 1970s brought forth much more specific research in media-based technology, and when one reviews the literature it is apparent the investigative methodology had become more refined. Key investigative themes included the following.

Media Inquiry: Family and Society
- How "programmable" are children under the influence of media-based technologies? What factors affect the selection and assimilation of attitudes and values? What conditions might allow motion media to become a more

powerful means of value indoctrination than parents or educators?

- What is the likelihood of the establishment of a media elite? How powerful and influential might such a media elite become? Who or what becomes most responsible for our perception of the world and world events?
- How are children influenced by the amount of fantasy present in media presentation?
- How much exposure to media-based technology is too much exposure?

It had been suggested by some that the value of information and its relation to life experience was being reduced by media-based technologies. Concerns relative to both the quantity of information delivered by technology, the quality of information as accumulated and delivered in programmed form, and the control over the distribution of information were debated.

Some believed that there might arise those who would irreverently manipulate media technologies as a channel for information control. Others sensed the access to instant information and communication via motion media technology brought with it a reduced appreciation for the richness, contradiction, and complexity to be found in people, circumstances, and events.

Research Snapshots

❏ **Starkey and Swinford**. Starkey and Swinford continued the tradition of investigating the displacement effects of media by focusing on their impact on children's reading habits outside of school. They surveyed 226 fifth and sixth grade students divided into five groups stratified by reading ability. They found that:

- Media displaced reading more frequently among poor readers than better readers.
- Displacement effects seemed negatively related to intellectual level (Starkey and Swinford, 1974).

33

❑ **Harvey Lesser**. In his book on television and preschool children, Lesser (1977) suggested that unaided exposure to motion media is much less effective than assisted or guided exposure. With guided exposure, understanding of program content is enhanced by the motivational aspects of media. While Lesser praised the potential benefits of media, he also raised concerns about a child's attention span in relation to media-based presentations:

■*Dual attending:* To what extent can children focus upon multiple information sources?

■How difficult is it for children to discern incidental messages from intended messages?

■To what degree do children follow extended messages or story lines?

❑ **Michael Howe**. Howe's 1977 media-based research addressed both developmental and cognitive issues. *Summary of findings and inferences:*

■A child's immature self-identification presumes certain incapabilities in distinguishing between elements of fantasy and reality.

■Rather than being passive recipients of information generated by media-based presentation, children assimilate and comprehend information based on prior knowledge and interest.

■Experience influences how and why humans selectively attend to some information they receive, while ignoring, forgetting, or distorting other information.

■Information that is distorted may have more to do with the preconceptions established in prior knowledge than inaccurate or inefficient delivery of information via a media-based technology.

❑ **Marie Winn**. Media-based technology was scrutinized for two unique phenomena in the middle 1970s. Skeptics of electronic technologies in learning argued that children may suffer from *media trance*, in which television viewing creates an environment leading to sensory assault and overload. In an effort to achieve homeostasis, children respond to television by "shutting down" various sensory or attention mechanisms and inevitably become passive (Winn, 1977). Such assertions have never been substantiated, and seem contrary to attention models in information processing theory.

Motion media technologies have also been accused of causing--or at least contributing to--hyperactivity in children.

The constant shifting of visual imagery is seen as related to hyperkinetic syndrome, because a subject's reference point must shift second to second. It was suggested that the accelerated pace of media-based materials "programmed" shorter attention spans in children. Some hypothesized that a hyperactive child attempts to recapture the dynamic qualities found in media by rapidly changing their perceptual orientations, thus contributing to frantic or hyperkinetic behavior (Dumont, 1976). Sensory overload theories became the basis for such hypotheses, suggesting that children who are not developmentally equipped to handle fast-paced electronic stimulation may react behaviorally by exhibiting an increase in crankiness and irritability (Winn, 1977). Winn suggested that such negative behaviors are not deliberate, purposeful, or within a child's active control. Such behavioral demonstrations are more akin to the crankiness or irritability of a child waking from sleep. Winn encouraged further research be done pertinent to "states of consciousness" during exposure to media-based presentation. Currently there are no significant studies that support the notion that electronic technologies promote hyperactivity in children.

❑ **Ellen Wartella**. Wartella pointed to three cognitive prerequisites to the efficient understanding and comprehension of content in motion media:
 ▪The ability to select consequential information and *disregard* extraneous data;
 ▪The ability to *order* consequential information into essential themes;
 ▪The ability to *draw inferences* that go beyond what may be explicitly presented.
Wartella warned that the analysis of children's comprehension of media-based material must include not only an evaluation of explicit meaning but also careful analysis of implied information as well.
Summary of findings:
 ▪Comprehension is often incomplete and fragmentary in media-based presentation of dramatic story material.
 ▪Recall of essential material relevant to understanding a story plot varies with respect to age and developmental maturity.
  -Grade two children recalled only 66% of the material adults judged essential in plot construction.
  -Grade five students recalled 84% of the essential material.

-Grade eight students recalled 92% of the material
adults judged as essential.

▪Understanding of interrelationships among central
events decreases with younger subjects.

Research Histories: 1980's

Research Snapshot

❑ **Kate Moody**. A text summarizing many of the societal
concerns regarding the impact of long-term exposure to
motion media in the home environment appeared in the early
1980s. It addressed the following issues, many of which
were not new, but of continuing concern (Moody, 1980):

▪To what extent may motion media overstimulate a
child's mind? What are the implications for sensory overload
in motion media?

▪What influence does motion media have on play
behavior, especially as television may replace play behavior
in familial environments?

▪To what extent does motion media foster nonintegrated
knowledge? Does media-based information lack sufficient
context clues for the accurate comprehension of content in
context?

▪Is there a correlation between the amount of motion
media exposure and a reduction in attention span in
children?

▪As exposure to motion media increases, does the use of
text based materials decrease?

Research Histories: 1990's

Research Snapshot

Contemporary Questions and Issues. It is
interesting to note that, as we explore emerging
technologies such as multi-media, interactive
television, the Internet, and virtual reality, many of
the questions which first arose in the 1950's
remain appropriate to the 1990's.

Media Inquiry: Family and Society

We have compiled a list of questions that are
currently being pondered by sociologists and
educational psychologists (Rivard, 1995). Check
those that seem familiar to you based on our

research review. Consider current Internet technology. From a personal and subjective point of view, what are your opinions on the following topics?

- ❑ Which "needs" are met by increased exposure to technology?
- ❑ Which "needs" may be deprived as a result of increased technologic exposure?
- ❑ What will be the overall cumulative effect of media-based technologies on children?
- ❑ What do families "give up" in order to engage in technologic intercourse?
- ❑ Will the media and information technologies available cause children to become "prematurely" mature?
- ❑ What is the impact of technology on familial, social, and peer interactions?
- ❑ To what extent does technology become a narcotic for people who defer investment in human relations to technologically surrogate relationships?
- ❑ How and to what extent will adults and children discern reality from virtual realities?
- ❑ To what extent will we rely upon technology as an escapist mechanism? When is this healthy, when is it unhealthy?
- ❑ How does technology influence our world view?
- ❑ To what extent might we be "programmed" by technologic managers?
- ❑ Under what conditions are media-based presentations a powerful means of value indoctrination?

References

Dumont, M. (1976). Letter from Matthew Dumont. *American Journal of Psychiatry*, 133 (April).

Heinich, R., Molenda, M., & Russell, J. (1993). *Instructional Media and the New Technologies of Instruction* (4th ed.). New York: Macmillan.

Himmelweit, H. (1958). *Television and the Child*. London: Oxford University Press.

Howe, M. (1977). *Television and Children*. Hamden: Linnet Books.

Lesser, H. (1977). *Television and the Preschool Child*. New York: Academic Press.

Moody, K. (1980). *Growing Up on Television*. New York: Times Books.

Rivard, J. (1995). *Select Topics on Technology, Teaching, & Learning*. Needham Heights: Simon & Schuster.

Starkey, J. & Swinford, H. (1974). Reading? Does Television Viewing Time Affect It? Northern Illinois University, ED 090-966.

Wartella, E. (1979). *Children Communicating: Media Development of Thought, Speech, and Understanding*. Beverly Hills: Sage Publishing.

Winn, M. (1977). *The Plug-in Drug*. New York: Viking Press.

Part Five: Your Address Book

World Wide Web Resources for Sociologists

(*Instructor*: URL's frequently change or disappear. If you can't find a site, use one of the search engines listed below to look for it by name.)

NOTE: For an expanded list of related sites, see the following:
http://www.abacon.com/sociology/hotlinks/sochot.html
Allyn & Bacon's Sociology Hot Links.

http://www.abacon.com/sociology/soclinks/index.html
Allyn & Bacon's Sociology Links

http://www.prenhall.com/~bookbind/pubbooks/henslin
Henslin's Sociology, 3/e (See WebDestinations for each chapter)

General Useful Sites
http://www.georgetown.edu/crossroads/asw
American Studies Web

http://www.digital-cafe.com/~webmaster/begin00.html
Beginners Central Internet Tutorial

http://www.edoc.com/ejournal
EJournal: Links to Electronic Journals

http://www.sandia.gov/sci_compute/html_ref.html
HTML Reference Manual

http://www.vir.com/~sher/julian.htm
Investigative Journalism (Guide to the Internet)

http://www.loc.gov
Library of Congress

Search Engines
http://www.altavista.digital.com
AltaVista Search

http://www.excite.com
Excite Netsearch

http://www.lycos.com
Lycos Search

http://webcrawler.com
WebCrawler Search

http://www.yahoo.com/search.html
Yahoo Search

General Sociology Sites

http://www.asanet.org
American Sociological Association

http://www.asanet.org/undergra.htm
ASA Section on Undergraduate Education

http://www.bbp.com/bbp/resource.html
Brown & Benchmark's Social Science Web Resources

http://link.bubl.ac.uk/sociology
BUBL Links: Sociology

http://www.uku.fi/departments/sociology/socio.htm
dredNET Sociology Server

http://www.einet.net/galaxy/Social-Sciences/Sociology.
html
Galaxy Guide to Sociology

http://www.ucm.es/OTROS/isa
International Sociological Association

http://www.princeton.edu/~sociolog/links.html
Princeton's Sociology Links

http://www.lib.lehigh.edu/socsciences/sociol.html
Lehigh University Sociology Web Server Listing

http://risya3.hus.osaka-u.ac.jp/Links/linksE.html
Osaka University Links to Sociology in Japan

http://coombs.anu.edu.au/CoombswebPages/
EJrnls-Register.html

Register of Social Science E-Journals
http://www.mnsfld.edu/depts/lib/mu-scref.html
Social Science Ready Reference

http://www.socabs.org
Sociological Abstracts Home Page

http://www.trinity.edu/~mkearl/index.html
Sociological Tour of Cyberspace

http://www.wam.umd.edu/~allan/Welcome.html
The Sociology Corner

http://www.mcmaster.ca/socscidocs/socnet.htm
Sociology Courses on the Internet

http://www.ssc.wisc.edu/~myers/cbsm/socdept.htm
Sociology Departments Web Pages

http://www.w3.org/pub/DataSources/bySubject/
Sociology/Listserv.txt
Sociology Listservs

http://hakatai.mcli.dist.maricopa.edu/smc/ml/sociology.
html
Sociology Places to Explore

http://www3.fullerton.edu/hss/Sociology/links.htm
Sociology Sites on the Web

http://www.pscw.uva.nl/sociosite
SocioSite: Going Dutch Sociology

http://www.socioweb.com/~markbl/socioweb/index.
html
The SocioWeb Sociological Resource Center

http://sosig.esrc.bris.ac.uk
SOSIG: Social Science Information Gateway

http://147.26.186.101/areas/socres.htm
Southwest Texas State Sociology and Internet
Resources

http://www.uni-koeln.de/wiso-fak/soziologiesem/
internet/sources.html
Soziologie im Internet (Only in German)

http://www.lemoyne.edu/ts/7tsmain.html
Teaching Sociology homepage

http://www.lib.berkeley.edu/GSSI/sociolog.html
U.C. Berkeley Libraries: Sociology

http://socsci.colorado.edu/SOC/RES
U. Colorado's WWW Resources for Sociologists

http://www.umsl.edu/~sociolog/resource.htm
U. Missouri-St. Louis Sociology Links

http://www.arts.su.edu.au/Arts/departs/social/links.html
U. of Sydney Sociology Links

http://coombs.anu.edu.au/WWWVL-SocSci.html
WWW Virtual Library: Social Science

http://iridium.nttc.edu/gov_res.html
WWW Virtual Library: US Government Information
Sources

http://www.yahoo.com/Social_Science/Sociology
Yahoo: Sociology

Aging

http://www.aoa.dhhs.gov
Administration on Aging

http://www.shc.edu/aging.htm
Aging Groups and Organizations

http://www-lib.usc.edu/Info/Gero/dissert.htm
Andrus Gerontology Library: Dissertations On Aging

http://www-lib.usc.edu/Info/Gero/gerourl.htm
Andrus Gerontology Library: Web Sources on Aging

http://www.aoa.dhhs.gov/aoa/webres/craig.htm
AOA Directory of WEB and Gopher Sites on Aging

http://www.aoa.dhhs.gov/aoa/pages/jpostlst.html
AOA Internet and E-mail Resources on Aging

http://www.asanet.org/aging.htm
ASA Section on Sociology of Aging

http://www.clearinghouse.net/inter/1129.html
Clearinghouse: Aging, Gerontology, Old Age

http://lamar.colostate.edu/~barberhd/links.htm
Clifton E. Barber's Links to Web Sites on Aging and
Gerontology

http://www.aoa.dhhs.gov/aoa/pages/jpostlst.html
E-mail and Internet Resources on Aging

http://www.gen.emory.edu/medweb/medweb.geriatrics.
html
MedWeb: Geriatrics Links

http://WWW.Trinity.Edu/~mkearl/geron.html
Resources in Social Gerontology

http://www.lawinfo.com/forum/age.html
Recent Developments in Age Discrimination Law

http://www.geron.uga.edu/agesites.html
U. Georgia Gerontology Center Aging Related Web
Sites

http://www.aoa.dhhs.gov/aoa/webres/craig.htm
WEB and Gopher Sites on Aging

http://www.yahoo.com/Health/Geriatrics_and_Aging
Yahoo: Geriatrics and Aging

Applied Sociology
http://www.asanet.org/practice.htm
ASA Section on Sociological Practice

http://www.stat.ucla.edu/journals/er
Evaluation Review: Journal of Applied Social Research

http://www.indiana.edu/~appsoc
Society for Applied Sociology

http://kennedy.soc.surrey.ac.uk/socresonline
Sociological Research Online (J. of Applied Sociology)

Collective Behavior and Social Movements
http://paul.spu.edu/~sinnfein/berlet.html
Armed Militias, Right Wing Populism, and
Scapegoating (Article)

http://www.ssc.wisc.edu/~myers/cbsm
ASA Section on Collective Behavior and Social
Movements

http://www.ssc.wisc.edu/~myers/cbsm/active.htm
Collective Behavior and Social Movements: Activist
Links

http://www.ssc.wisc.edu/~myers/cbsm/teach.htm
Collective Behavior and Social Movements: Teaching
Resources

http://www.well.com/user/srhodes/militia.html
Information on Militias (Links)

http://www.stile.lut.ac.uk/~gyobs/GLOBAL/t0000087.
html
Globe Resources: Social Movements Of Indigenous
Peoples

http://www.militia-watchdog.org/m1.htm
Neo-Militia Links

http://lucy.ukc.ac.uk/csacpub/russian/mamay.html
Theories of Social Movements

Activist Groups
http://www.interactivism.com/docs/support.html
Activist Links

http://www.organic.com/Non.profits/Amnesty/index.html
Amnesty International

http://www.cures-not-wars.org
Cures Not Wars Online

http://www.famm.org
Families Against Mandatory Minimums

http://www.uaw.org/internet/acgroups.html
Good Groups: Fighting for Justice Activist Groups

http://www.igc.org/igc
IGC's Communities of Activists and Organizations

http://www.usa.net/uclr
Legal Justice Reform Network

http://www.phrf.org/index.html
Parliamentary Human Rights Foundation

http://www.vtw.org/others
Voters Telecommunications Watch

Criminology, Deviance, and Criminal Justice
http://www.acjnet.org/acjnet
Access to Justice Network (Canadian)

http://www.acjnet.org/textbase.html
ACJNet Justice Databases (Canada)

http://www.abanet.org
American Bar Association

http://www.bsos.umd.edu/asc
American Society of Criminology

http://www.asanet.org/crime.htm
ASA Section on Crime, Law, and Deviance

http://www.ccsa.ca
Canadian Centre on Substance Abuse

http://www.courttv.com
CourtTV Law Center

http://ourworld.compuserve.com/homepages/ISCPP/
Page10.htm
Crime Prevention Website Links

http://sun.soci.niu.edu/~critcrim
The Critical Criminology (American Society of
Criminology)

http://www.ojp.usdoj.gov/bjs
FBI Crime Statistics

http://www.drcnet.org
Guided Tour of the War on Drugs

http://ilj.org/#cjserver
Institute for Law & Justice (Links)

http://www.ilrg.com
International Legal Resources Guide

http://www.scj.albany.edu:90/jcjpc
Journal of Criminal Justice and Popular Culture

http://www.ncjrs.org
Justice Information Center

http://www.lec.org
Life Education Links on Drugs, Violence, and AIDS
Prevention

http://www.nida.nih.gov/NIDAHome.html
National Institute on Drug Abuse (NIDA)

http://www.nvc.org
National Victim Center

http://www.health.org/pubs/95hhs/ar18txt.htm
NCADI: 1995 National Household Drug Abuse Survey

www.pavnet.org
PAVNET: Partners Against Violence

http://www.health.org
Prevline Substance Abuse Page

http://www.igc.apc.org/justice/prisons/resources.html
Prison-related Internet Resources

http://www.creative.net/~penet
Prostitutes' Education Network (Links)

http://www.ncjrs.org/unojust
United Nations Crime and Justice Clearinghouse

http://weedseed.ilj.org
Weed and Seed: Reclaiming America's Neighborhoods

http://www.yahoo.com/society_and_culture/crime
Yahoo: Crime

Juvenile Delinquency
http://www2.deepcove.com/cry/cr_indx.html
CRY: Crime, Responsibility and Youth Index

http://www.ncjrs.org/jjwww.htm
Juvenile Justice WWW Sites

http://www.ncjrs.org/ojjdp/html/news.html
Office of Juvenile Justice News and Resources

http://www.agnr.umd.edu/users/nnfr/yvp_sig.html
Youth Violence Prevention

Culture
http://rs6.loc.gov
American Memory from the Library of Congress

http://pantheon.cis.yale.edu/~rmelende/culture.online.
html
ASA Culture Section: Culture Online

http://www.asanet.org/culture.htm
ASA Section on Sociology of Culture

http://darkwing.uoregon.edu/~caps
Center For Asian and Pacific Studies

http://www.dnai.com:80/~rutledge/CHCP_home.html
Chinese Historical and Cultural Project

http://www.nrsbgym.dk/engelsk/theory.html
Cultural Studies and Critical Theory

http://www1.nisiq.net/~jsengine/eng/society/index.htm
Japan: Culture & Society

http://curry.edschool.virginia.edu/go/multicultural
The Multicultural Pavilion at the University of Virginia

http://www.blender.com/blender1.1/digest/popspeak/
popspeak1.html
Popspeak: Popular Culture Vocabulary

http://www.maxwell.syr.edu/nativeweb
NativeWeb: Earth's Indigenous People

http://www.eerie.fr/~alquier/Cyber/culture.html
Net Tribes: Future Culture

http://edward.cprost.sfu.ca/438/index.html
Pacific Waves Journal: Comparing Canadian and
Australian Culture

http://www.ulst.ac.uk/services/library/ni/research/
research.htm
Register of Research on Northern Ireland

http://www.tribal.com/resour.htm
Tribal Voice: Native American Resources

http://ucsu.colorado.edu/~jsu/launcher.html
The Ultimate Jewish/Israel Link Launcher

http://www.worldculture.com
The Web of Culture

Demography, Population and Urbanization
http://www.asanet.org/commun.htm
ASA Section on Community and Urban Sociology

http://www.asanet.org/intermig.htm
ASA Section on International Migration

http://www.asanet.org/populat.htm
ASA Section on Sociology of Population

http://www.hud.gov/nnw/nnwindex.html
Housing and Neighborhood Networks

http://www.well.com/user/cmty
Intentional Communities

http://www.solbaram.org/indexes/cmmuni.html
Manfred Davidman on Community

http://www.ncl.org/ncl
National Civic League

http://www.cais.com/nlc
National League of Cities

http://opr.princeton.edu/archive
Office of Population Research Data Archive

http://popindex.princeton.edu
Office of Population Research Population Index

http://www.pop.psu.edu
Population Research Institute

http://www.psc.lsa.umich.edu/DA/index.html
Population Studies Center Data Archive

http://www.mta.ca/rstp
Rural and Small Town Programme

http://www.lapop.lsu.edu/rss
Rural Sociology Society

http://www.census.gov/sdc/www
State Data Centers (Population)

http://www.urban.org
The Urban Institute

http://usacitylink.com
USA CityLink Home Page

http://www.census.gov
U.S Census Bureau

http://cedr.lbl.gov/mdocs/LBL_census.html
U.S. Census Data at Lawrence Berkeley National
Laboratory

http://www.ciesin.org/datasets/us-demog/
us-demog-home.html
U.S. Demography

http://www.census.gov/cgi-bin/gazetteer
U.S. Gazetteer

http://coombs.anu.edu.au/ResFacilities/
DemographyPage.html
WWW Virtual Library: Demography & Population
Studies

The Economy

http://www.princeton.edu/~orgoccwk
ASA Section on Organizations, Occupations, and Work

http://www.asanet.org/polecon.htm
ASA Section on Political Economy of the World
Systems

http://www.econ.ag.gov
Economic Research Service

http://www.epn.org
Electronic Policy Network

http://www.law.cornell.edu/topics/
employment_discrimination.html
Employment Discrimination Law

http://violet.berkeley.edu/~iir
Institute of Industrial Relations

http://janweb.icdi.wvu.edu
Job Accommodation Network

http://www.igc.apc.org/labornet
LaborNet

http://www.solbaram.org/indexes/ecnmcs.html
Manfred Davidman on Economics

http://www.urban.org/periodcl/prr25_1b.htm
Widening Wage Inequality

http://www.woa.org/links.htm
Workers of America Links

Education

http://www.aacc.nche.edu
American Association of Community Colleges

http://ericir.syr.edu
Ask ERIC Education Information

http://www.aspeninst.org
Aspen Institute for Leadership Education

http://www.asanet.org/educat.htm
ASA Section on Sociology of Education

http://cause-www.colorado.edu
Cause: Managing and Using Information Higher
Education Resources

http://edreform.com
The Center for Education Reform

http://www.col.org
Commonwealth of Learning Using Distance
Communication

http://www.ed.gov
Department of Education

http://www.ed.gov/EdRes/EdRes.html
Department of Education: Resources

http://oeri.ed.gov:8888/STATES/direct/SF
Department of Education: State Resources Database

51

http://www.du.org
Diversity University (MOO provider)

http://education.acad.emich.edu/green/Resources.html
Education Resources

http://eric-web.tc.columbia.edu
ERIC Clearinghouse on Urban Education Web

http://andromeda.tradewave.com/galaxy/
Social-Sciences/Education.html
Galaxy Social Science Education Resources

http://www.gnacademy.org:8001/HyperNews/get/talk/
index.html
Global Network Academy Distance Education Guide

http://uttou2.to.utwente.nl
International Association for Evaluation of Educational
Achievement

http://www.cgcs.org
National Council of the Great City Schools

http://govinfo.kerr.orst.edu/sddb-stateis.html
School District Data Book Profiles: 1989-1990

http://www.sunspace.com
School District Demographics (Subscription needed)

http://www.yahoo.com/Education
Yahoo: Education

The Environment
http://www.flnet.com/~tw/activism.htm
Activist Groups for Environmental Preservation (And
other groups)

http://www.asanet.org/environ.htm
ASA Section on Environment and Technology

http://www.ulb.ac.be:80/ceese
Centre for Economic and Social Studies on the
Environment

http://wwwgateway.ciesin.org/dataset-home.html
CIESIN Gateway Dataset Guides

http://www.sdsc.edu/ESA/ESA.htm
Ecological Society of America

http://www.igc.org/igc/econet/index.html
EcoNet

http://www.ecotrust.org
Ecotrust

http://www.envirolink.org/EnviroLink_Library
EnviroLink Library

http://www.igc.apc.org/eic
Environmental Information Center

http://govinfo.kerr.orst.edu
Government Information Sharing Project

http://www.mbnet.mb.ca/linkages
Linkages: Resources for Environment & Development
Policy Makers

http://www.cnie.org/nle/index.shtml
National Library for the Environment

http://www.cais.com/publish/links.htm
Science & the Environment Links

http://solstice.crest.org
Solstice: Sustainable Energy and Development Online!

http://www.seac.org
Student Environmental Action Coalition

http://www.yahoo.com/Society_and_Culture/
Environment_and_Nature/Organizations
Yahoo: Environment and Nature Organizations

http://www.yahoo.com/Business_and_Economy/
Products_and_Services/Magazines/Environment
Yahoo: Magazines on Environment

http://www.yahoo.com/Society_and_Culture/
Environment_and_Nature/Pollution/Activist_Groups
Yahoo: Pollution Activist Groups

http://www.yahoo.com/Society_and_Culture/
Environment_and_Nature/Pollution/Activist_Groups
Yahoo: Pollution Activist Groups (UK)

http://www.yahoo.com/Society_and_Culture/
Organizations/Public_Interest_Groups/Environment
Yahoo: Public Interest Groups: Environment

Ethics
http://www.ethics.ubc.ca/papers/AppliedEthics.html
Applied Ethics Resources on WWW

http://www.cre.gu.se/links
Centre for Research Ethics: Links to Related Sites

http://www.psych.bangor.ac.uk/DeptPsych/Ethics/
HumanResearch.html
Human Subjects and Research Ethics

http://www.mcb.co.uk/services/articles/liblink/intr/
ethics.htm
Robert Alun Jones, "The Ethics of Research in
Cyberspace"

The Family
http://www.asanet.org/family.htm
ASA Section on Family

http://www.tmn.com/cdf/links.html
Children's Defense Fund Links

http://www.acf.dhhs.gov
DHHS Administration for Children and Families

http://www.frc.org
The Family Research Council

http://www.familyvillage.wisc.edu/library.htm
Family Village Library

http://www.webring.org/cgi-bin/
webring?ring=singleparent&list
Single Parents sites

http://osiris.colorado.edu/SOC/RES/family.html
U. Colorado's Family Sociology Resources

Gender

http://www.aauw.org/4000/extlinks.html
AAUW: Other Websites of Interest

http://www.asanet.org/sexgend.htm
ASA Section on Sex and Gender

http://www.asanet.org/sexualit.htm
ASA Section on the Sociology of Sexualities

http://www.ibd.nrc.ca/~mansfield/feminism
Feminism and Women's Resources Page

http://www.igc.apc.org/women/feminist.html
Feminist Activist Resources on the Net

http://www.feminist.org/gateway/1_gatway.html
Feminist Gateway

http://www.well.com/user/freedom
Feminists For Free Expression

http://www.glaad.org/glaad/electronic/links.html
Gay and Lesbian Anti-Defamation Links

http://www.ngltf.org/ngltflink.html
Gay and Lesbian Links

http://english-server.hss.cmu.edu/Gender.html
Gender and Sexuality Links

http://www.ocs.mq.edu.au/~korman/feminism/
feminism.html
Kate Orman's Feminist Links

http://www.now.org/resource.html
National Organization of Women: Resources on the
Internet

http://rohan.sdsu.edu/faculty/huckle/research.html
Pat Huckle's Women's Studies Research Links

http://www.pleiades-net.com/lists/orgs.html
Pleiades Networks: Directory of Women's
Organizations & Resources

http://www.stir.ac.uk/socinfo/journal/journal1/j1_4.
html
Ruth Madigan, "Gender Issues: Teaching with
Computers in Sociology"

http://libweb.uoregon.edu/instruct/womenst.htm
U. Oregon's Guide to Feminist Research Methods

http://www.voiceofwomen.com/other.html
VOWworld: Other Internet Resources for Women

http://www.igc.org/igc/womensnet/index.html
WomensNet

http://www.feminist.com/reso.htm
Women's Resources and Links

http://www.ucc.uconn.edu/~wwwwmst/links.html
Women's Studies Links

http://www-unix.umbc.edu/~korenman/wmst/links.html
Women's Studies/Women's Issues WWW Sites

http://www.wwwomen.com
WWWomen! Search Directory for Women Online

http://www.vix.com/pub/men/index.html
WWW Virtual Library: Men's Issues Page

http://www.vix.com/pub/men/orgs/orgs.html
WWW Virtual Library: Men's Movement
Organizations

http://www.yahoo.com/Society_and_Culture/Gender
Yahoo: Gender

Medicine and Health

http://www.immunet.org/atn
AIDS Treatment News Archive

http://www.cancer.org/links.html
American Cancer Society Cancer Information
Resources

http://www.asanet.org/medical.htm
ASA Section on Medical Sociology

http://ash.org/otherweb/index.html
ASH Links to Smoking Related Sites

http://www.apiahf.org/apiahf
Asian and Pacific Islander American Health Forum

http://www.cdc.gov
Centers for Disease Control & Prevention

http://www.os.dhhs.gov
Department of Health and Human Services

http://www.hslib.washington.edu
HealthLinks

http://gilligan.mc.duke.edu/h-devil
Healthy Devil On-Line Health Topics

http://www.mol.net
Medicine Online Medical Related Sites

http://www.cdc.gov/nchswww/nchshome.htm
National Center for Health Statistics

http://www.best.com/~sirlou/medical.html
Sheimp's Medical Information Links

http://www.oneworld.org/unicef
UNICEF Home Page

http://www.who.ch
World Health Organization

http://www.yahoo.com/Health
Yahoo: Health

Media

http://www.vub.ac.be/SCOM/cemeso/index.html
Center for Media Sociology

http://www.december.com/cmc/mag
Computer Mediated Communication Magazine Index

http://www.uwindsor.ca/faculty/socsci/geog/mogy/ivsa/
ivsa.html
International Visual Sociology Association

http://www.justthink.org/links.htm
Just Think Foundation Media Links

http://www.uark.edu/depts/comminfo/www/
massmedia.html
Mass Media Culture

http://www.feminist.org/news/otherpub.html
News Media Online

http://www.mediahistory.com
The Media History Project

http://censored.sonoma.edu/ProjectCensored
Project Censored: News That Didn't Make the News

http://www.yahoo.com/News_and_Media
Yahoo: News and Media

News Media Online
http://cnn.com/DIGEST
CNN Digest

http://www.j-times.com
Irish Times

http://www.jpost.co.il
Jerusalem Post

http://www.mojones.com
Mojo Wire (Mother Jones)

http://www.npr.org
National Public Radio

http://nytimesfax.com
NY Times Fax

http://www.pbs.org
Public Broadcasting System (PBS) On Line

http://www.seatimes.com
Seattle Times

http://www.the-times.co.uk/news/pages/home.
html?000999
Times of London

http://www.usatoday.com
USA Today

http://www.yahoo.com/News_and_Media/Newspapers/
Indices
Yahoo: Newspaper Indices

Politics

http://www.anc.org.za
African National Congress Home Page

http://www.asanet.org/politic.htm
ASA Section on Political Sociology

http://www.asanet.org/law.htm
ASA Section on Sociology of Law

http://paul.spu.edu/~sinnfein/progressive.html
Brian's Progressive Pages (Political activist links)

http://www.c-span.org
C-SPAN

http://voter96.cqalert.com/Welcome.html
Congressional Quarterly's American Voter

http://www.gsa.gov/staff/pa/cic
Government Consumer Publications

http://www.lwv.org/~lwvus/altweb.html
League of Women Voters: Other WWW sites

http://www.whitehouse.gov/WH/
Independent_Agencies/html/independent_links.html
Links to Independent Federal Agencies & Commissions

http://infomanage.com/micconversion/default.html
Military Industrial Complex Links

http://www.politicalindex.com
National Political Index

http://www.oas.org
The Organization of American States

http://www.luna.nl/~benne/pp/index.htm
Political Parties and Youth Organizations Around the
World

http://www.agora.stm.it/politic
Political Resources on the Net

http://www.dreamscape.com/frankvad/us-gov.html
Virtual Tour of the US Government

http://www.vote-smart.org
Vote Smart Web

http://www.whitehouse.gov
The White House

http://www.yahoo.com/Government/Politics
Yahoo: Politics

http://www.yahoo.com/Society_and_Culture/
Organizations
Yahoo: Public Interest Groups

Poverty and Homelessness

http://csf.colorado.edu/homeless/index.html
Communications for a Sustainable Future Homeless
Resources

http://aspe.os.dhhs.gov/poverty/poverty.htm
Federal Poverty Guidelines for 1997

http://www.brown.edu/Departments/
World_Hunger_Program/hungerweb/researchers.html
HungerWeb: Researchers Entry Point

http://www.ssc.wisc.edu/irp
Institute for Research on Poverty

http://www.HomeAid.org/links.htm
Links to Homeless Information on the Internet

http://www.umich.edu/~socwk/poverty/links.html
Links to Poverty-Related Resources

http://nch.ari.net/direct1.html
National Coalition for the Homeless Directories

http://nch.ari.net/database.html
National Coalition for the Homeless Online Library

http://cpmcnet.columbia.edu/dept/nccp
National Center for Children in Poverty

http://www.epn.org/tcf/xxblue.html
Polarization of American Society (Article)

http://action.org/resources.html
Resources for Ending Poverty and Hunger

http://csf.colorado.edu/homeless/index.html
Communications for a Sustainable Future Homeless
Resources

http://www.reliefweb.int/resource/related.html
U.N. ReliefWeb Related Sites List

http://www.census.gov/pub/socdemo/www/povarea.
html
U.S. Census Bureau: Poverty Areas

http://www.census.gov/ftp/pub/hhes/www/poverty.html
U.S. Census Bureau: Poverty Statistics

http://www.iglou.com/why/whylink.htm
World Hunger Year's Hunger and Poverty Links

http://www.yahoo.com/Society_and_Culture/Poverty
Yahoo: Poverty

http://www.yahoo.com/Government/Politics/
Political_Issues/Welfare_Reform
Yahoo: Welfare Reform

Race and Ethnicity

http://www.asanet.org/latino.htm
ASA Section on Latino/a Sociology

http://www.asanet.org/raceeth.htm
ASA Section on Racial and Ethnic Minorities

http://eng.hss.cmu.edu/race
Carnegie Mellon Race Links

http://www.comp.lancs.ac.uk/sociology/research/errg.
html
Ethnic Minorities and Race Research Group

http://www.brad.ac.uk/bradinfo/research/eram/eram.
html
Ethnicity, Racism and the Media Programme (UK)

http://www.noi.org/finalcall
The Final Call: Black Community Issues and Events

http://fatty.law.cornell.edu/topics/civil_rights.html
Legal Information Institute: Civil Rights Law and
Discrimination

http://www.union.edu/computing/library/guide/mcafric.
html
Multicultural Resources: African-American/Africana
Studies

http://www.union.edu/computing/library/guide/mclat.
html
Multicultural Resources: Latino-American/Latin
American Studies

http://www.union.edu/computing/library/guide/mcna.
html
Multicultural Resources: Native Americans

http://www.mecca.org/~crights/ncrm.html
National Civil Rights Museum

http://www.ruu.nl/ercomer/nc/index.html
New Community: Journal of European Research Centre
on Migration and Ethnic Relations

http://http.tamu.edu:8000/~e303gt
Race and Ethnic Studies Institute

http://www.union.edu/computing/library/guide/
mcsources.html#Web
Schaffer Library Multicultural Resources: Web Sites

http://resi.tamu.edu/index.html
Texas A&M Race and Ethnic Studies Institute

http://WWW.Trinity.Edu/~mkearl/race.html
Trinity Sociology: Resources in Race and Ethnic
Studies

http://www.union.edu/computing/library/guide/
mcasia.html#Web
The Virtual Library: Asian Americans/East Asian
Studies

http://www.union.edu/computing/library/guide/
mcjewish.html#Web
The Virtual Library: Jewish Americans/Judaica

http://humanitas.ucsb.edu/shuttle/minority.html
Voice of the Shuttle: Minority Studies Page

http://www.ruu.nl/ercomer/wwwvl/index.html
WWW Virtual Library: Migration and Ethnic Relations

http://www.yahoo.com/Society_and_Culture/Cultures/
African_American/Organizations
Yahoo: African American Organizations

http://www.yahoo.com/Social_Science/
Migration_and_Ethnic_Relations
Yahoo: Migration and Ethnic Relations

http://www.yahoo.com/Society_and_Culture/
Race_Relations
Yahoo: Race Relations

Religion

http://www.asanet.org/religion.htm
ASA Section on the Sociology of Religion

http://student.uq.edu.au/~py101663/zentry1.htm
Cult Awareness & Information Centre - Australia

http://library.uwaterloo.ca/discipline/religious/
discussions.html
Electronic Discussion Groups in Religious Studies

http://ftp.qrd.org/qrd/www/rrr/rrrpage.html
Fighting the Radical Religious Right (Useful links)

http://world.std.com/~awolpert
General Theory of Religion

http://www.psu.edu:80/jbe/resource.html
Global Resources for Buddhist Studies

http://www.religioustolerance.org/topicndx.htm
Index of Religious Links

http://shamash.org/trb/judaism.html
Judaism and Jewish Resources

http://socsci.colorado.edu/~brumbaug/CHURCH/RES/news.htm
Links to Religious Publications

http://www.stile.lut.ac.uk/~gyobs/GLOBAL/t0000057.html
New Religious Movements: Resources

http://www.stile.lut.ac.uk/~gyobs/GLOBAL/t0000120.html
New Religious Movements: Web Sites

http://www.religioustolerance.org
Ontario Consultants on Religious Tolerance (Many links)

http://138.202.168.1/ethics/group8/abortion.html
Views On Abortion From Major Religious Groups

Research Methods and Statistics
http://www.asanet.org/math.htm
ASA Section on Mathematical Sociology

http://lion.icpsr.umich.edu/methsect
ASA Section on Methods

http://fdncenter.org
The Foundation Center (Grants)

http://odwin.ucsd.edu/glossary
Glossary of Social Science Computer and Social Science Data Terms

http://www.mcb.co.uk/liblink/intr/jourhome.htm
Internet Research Journal

http://www.parnet.org
PARnet: The Cornell Participatory Action Research Network

http://www.nova.edu/ssss/QR/index.html
The Qualitative Report

http://www.carleton.ca/~cmckie/research.html
Research Engines for the Social Sciences

http://www.soc.surrey.ac.uk/socresonline
Sociological Research Online

Databanks and Providers
http://www.cwu.edu/~asdc/home.html
Applied Social Data Center Home page

http://zeus.mzes.uni-mannheim.de/datasets
Eurobarometer

http://www.icpsr.umich.edu/gss
General Social Survey

http://www.isleuth.com
The Internet Sleuth (Links to 2000+ databases)

http://ssdc.ucsd.edu/ssdc/catalog.html
UCSD Data Collection

http://www.medaccess.com/census/census_s.htm
U.S. Statistical Abstract

Statistics
http://www.spss.com
SPSS Inc.

http://www.lib.umich.edu/libhome/Documents.center/
stsoc.html
Statistical Resources on the Web: Sociology

http://www.cheme.cmu.edu:80/usr/wh14/web/stat/
staintro.html#
Statistics: A Primer for Lawyers

http://www.stat.ucla.edu/jndex.phtml
UCLA Statistics Homepage

Social Change
http://www.sustainable.doe.gov
DOE's Center of Excellence for Sustainable
Development

http://www.stile.lut.ac.uk/~gyedb/STILE/t0000459.
html
Ed Brown's Resource Information: Global Change

http://cfn.cs.dal.ca/Environment/SCN/CommLink/
SCN-netguide.html
Internet Resources on Sustainability

http://web.1-888.com/longwave
Longwave and Social Cycles Resource Centre

http://www.soros.org/orlvnt.html
Open Society Web Sites

http://www.igc.apc.org/pbi
Peace Brigades International

http://www.igc.apc.org/pbi/links.html
Peace Brigades International: Web links

http://www.webhelp.com/future.htm
Project 21st Century

http://www.soros.org
Soros Foundations Network for Open Society

http://humnet.humberc.on.ca/t2-res.htm
Talk 2000 Resources

Social Psychology

http://www.asanet.org/socpsych.htm
ASA Section on Social Psychology

http://www.asanet.org/children.htm
ASA Section on the Sociology of Children

http://www.asanet.org/emotions.htm
ASA Section on Sociology of Emotions

http://journals.eecs.qub.ac.uk/BPS/BJSP/BJSP.html
The British Journal of Social Psychology

http://www.uiowa.edu/~grpproc/crisp/crisp.html
Current Research in Social Psychology

http://paradigm.soci.brocku.ca:80/~lward
George's Page (George Herbert Mead)

http://www.uwsp.edu/acad/psych/tpersoc.htm
Psychology: Personality & Social Links

http://server.bmod.athabascau.ca/html/aupr/social.htm
Social Psychology Links (Psychological perspective)

http://www.wesleyan.edu/psyc/psyc260
Social Psychology Network (Psychological perspective)

http://spsp.clarion.edu/spsp/SPSP.HTM
Society for Personality and Social Psychology

http://www.trinity.edu/~mkearl/socpsy.html
A Sociological Social Psychology

Social Stratification
http://www.pscw.uva.nl/sociosite/CLASS/bibA.html
Albert Benschop's Alphabetical Bibliography on Social
Class

http://www.asanet.org/rgc.htm
ASA Section on Race, Gender, and Class

http://fswinfo.fsw.ruu.nl/soc/HG/ismf
International Stratification and Mobility File

http://risya3.hus.osaka-u.ac.jp/shigeto/ssm/ssmE.html
Social Stratification and Mobility Survey (Japan)

**(Also see entries under Gender, Poverty and
Homelessness, and Race and Ethnicity)**

Social Structure and Social Interaction
http://www.asanet.org/orgoccup.htm
ASA Section on Organizations, Occupations, and Work

http://www.stile.lut.ac.uk/~gyobs/GLOBAL/t0000095.
html
Core and Periphery in World Systems Analysis

http://www.stile.lut.ac.uk/~gyedb/STILE/t0000460.
html
Ed Brown's Resource Information: Capitalism

http://www.stile.lut.ac.uk/~gyedb/STILE/t0000425.
html
Ed Brown's Resource Information: Development
Theory

http://www.stile.lut.ac.uk/~gyedb/STILE/index.html
Ed Brown's Political Economy Archive

http://www.stile.lut.ac.uk/~gyedb/STILE/t0000455.
html
Ed Brown's Resource Information: Neo-marxism

http://www.mpi-fg-koeln.mpg.de:80/~lk/netvis.html
A Gallery of Social Structures: Network Visualization

http://www.mpi-fg-koeln.mpg.de
Max Planck Institute for the Study of Societies

http://csf.Colorado.EDU/wsystems
The World-Systems Conferencing Electronic Network

Sociological Theory

http://csf.colorado.edu/psn/marxist-sociology/index.
html
ASA Section on Marxist Sociology

http://www.asanet.org/rational.htm
ASA Section on Rational Choice Theory

http://www.asanet.org/theory.htm
ASA Section on Theory

http://www.kutztown.edu/~ehrensal/ahshome.html
Association for Humanist Sociology

http://www.well.com/user/theory
The Common Theory Project

http://www2.uchicago.edu/jnl-crit-inq
Critical Theory-Driven Inquiry

http://diogenes.baylor.edu/WWWproviders/
Larry_Ridener/DSS/DEADSOC.HTML
Dead Sociologists' Society

http://www.lang.uiuc.edu/RelSt/Durkheim/
DurkheimHome.html
Durkheim Pages

http://www.comp.lancs.ac.uk/sociology/research/
ethnonews/ethnonews5/ethnonews5.html
Ethnomethodology and Conversation Newsletter

http://csf.Colorado.edu/psn/marx
The Marx/Engels Internet Archive

http://english-www.hss.cmu.edu/marx
Marx and Engels' Writings

http://www.wam.umd.edu/~allan/mcdonald.html
McDonaldization Home Page

http://www.usyd.edu.au/su/social/elias/elias.html
Norbert Elias and Process Sociology

http://jefferson.village.virginia.edu/pmc/contents.all.
html
Postmodern Culture

http://ernie.lang.nagoya-u.ac.jp/~miura/
Postmodern_Sites
Postmodernism in cyberspace

http://sun.soci.niu.edu/~sssi
Society for the Study of Symbolic Interaction

http://jefferson.village.virginia.edu/~spoons
Spoon Collective for Discussion of Philosophical Issues

Technology and Computers
http://apt.org/apt/index.html
Alliance for Public Technology

http://www.asanet.org/science.htm
ASA Section on Science, Knowledge, and Technology

http://www.asanet.org/computer.htm
ASA Section on Sociology and Computers

http://www.apc.org
Association for Progressive Communications

http://www.sscnet.ucla.edu/soc/csoc
Center for the Study of Online Communities

http://snyside.sunnyside.com/home
Computer Professionals for Social Responsibility

http://www.ctheory.com
CTHEORY: Journal of Technology and Culture

http://www.gn.apc.org/sgr
Scientists for Global Responsibility

http://www.lsu.edu:80/guests/ssss/public_html
Society for the Social Studies of Science

http://www.arts.ucsb.edu:80/~speed
SPEED: Technology, Media, Society

http://www.iit.edu/~livewire
Street-Level Live Wire: Communications Technology
for Youth

Violence and Abuse
http://www.asanet.org/peacewar.htm
ASA Section on Peace and War

http://www.netizen.org/Progressive/bcifv/links.html
B.C. Institute on Family Violence: Related Links

http://www.sunlink.net/~browning/index.htm#home
Child Abuse & Fatality Resource Guide

http://mail.med.upenn.edu/~jstoller/abuse.html
Child Abuse Links

http://www.igc.apc.org/conflictnet
ConflictNet: Conflict Resolution Resources

http://www.fvpf.org/fund/resources/sites.html
Domestic Peace Links

http://www.athens.net/~rblum/dvpindex.html
Domestic Violence Links

http://www.ocs.mq.edu.au/~korman/feminism/vaw.
html
Kate Orman's Violence Against Women Page

http://www.umn.edu/~mincava
Minnesota Higher Education Center Against Violence
and Abuse

http://www.exnet.iastate.edu/Pages/nncc/Abuse/
abuse.links.html
National Network for Child Care: Child Abuse Links

http://www.igc.apc.org/ni
Nonviolence International

http://www.cybergrrl.com/dv.html
SafetyNet Domestic Violence Resources

http://www.owens.com/tradescp/tg.html
Terrorist Group Profiles

http://www.yahoo.com/Society_and_Culture/Children/
Child_Abuse/Organizations
Yahoo: Child Abuse Organizations

Part Six: Activities

Henslin's Sociology: A Down to Earth Approach (3/e)

Chapter 1: The Sociological Perspective

1. [**Instructor**: Visit the Dead Sociologists Society for an excellent group project]. After reading the section, "The Development of Sociology," visit the Dead Sociologists Society (http://diogenes.baylor. edu/WWWproviders/Larry_Ridener/DSS/DEADSOC. HTML) and select one of the people discussed in the text. Gather material for a report on the sociologist's personal background, ideas, and writing. Present your findings to the class as part of a panel discussion on early sociologists. (If you can't access the site--it may have moved--go to one of the following search engines and enter the words DEAD SOCIOLOGISTS. Some search engine addresses are:

http://www.altavista.digital.com
http://www.excite.com
http://www.lycos.com
http://webcrawler.com

2. After reading the section "Applied and Clinical Sociology" and the box, "Sociologists at Work: What Applied Sociologists Do," browse the National Coalition for the Homeless home page and its links (http://nch.ari.net). Write a one-page paper addressing the following: If you were a sociologist working for the Coalition, what specific concerns might you consider? What kinds of uniquely sociological perspectives might you have to offer? (This early in the course, your thinking will necessarily be very general.)

Chapter 2: Culture

1. Freedom is a core value in United States society. Compare the eleven excerpts from "Declarations on Religious freedom" (found at http://www.kosone.com/people/ocrt/humright.htm). Write a one or two page report about common principles and differences found. Do people in our society agree on what religious freedom means? Do you think this core value is changing?

2. Search the Internet for information on a value conflict by accessing one of the following "search engines," and entering the word "abortion" in the search term blank.

> http://www.altavista.digital.com
> http://www.excite.com
> http://www.lycos.com
> http://webcrawler.com

Go to several of the sites and see whether you can determine the major arguments held by the pro-life and pro-choice sides. Prepare a written or oral report on your findings. To what extent does the disagreement indicate changes in core values in our society?

Chapter 3: Socialization

1. Child-rearing and child-care practices vary widely in different societies, and no less so within highly complex industrial societies. Explore some of these differences on the Internet. Use one of the following search engines and enter the search term, "child rearing." You might also try "child care." See what varieties of values and practices within the U. S. you can discover. Can you identify any of the social characteristics of those proposing a particular point of view? Try the same exercise by looking at different countries. Look at the term after the last address "dot" (for example, www.ucalg.ca). You might try ca (Canada), uk (England), au (Australia) for a start. Japan (jp) is interesting if you can find text in English. Be prepared to share your findings with the class in whatever form your instructor assigns. The search engines:

> http://www.altavista.digital.com
> http://www.excite.com
> http://www.lycos.com
> http://webcrawler.com

2. What can you discover about childhood socialization by examining children's games and pastimes? Explore this question by looking at children's pages on the Internet. Some starting places containing lists of sites include:

●HUGE List: Kid Stuff (http://thehugelist.com)
●Ryan Hackett's Kids' Pages: Animals, science, fun and games (http://seamonkey.ed.asu.edu/~gail/ryanpage. htm)
●Berit's Best Sites for Children (http://www.cochran. com/theosite/KSITES.html)

What is the relationship between childhood socialization and play? What are the children learning? What do they want to learn? Are the answers to these questions what you expected? Are they what you think traditional wisdom in our society says about children?

Chapter 4: Social Structure and Social Interaction

1. The power of the media, including the Internet, is raising new questions about control. Since the 1996 Telecommunications bill became law, treatment of censorship issues has exploded in both fervor and the volume of input. Use the AltaVista search engine (http://www.altavista. digital.com) to explore with the search word, "censorship." What are the issues? What are the arguments of those taking stands? What do you think? Prepare a written or oral report on your findings and opinions.

2. The creation of "intentional communities" represents a recent attempt to restore *Gemeinschaft* to modern living. Access the list of Intentional Communities of the WEB (http://www.well.com/user/ cmty/index.html) and browse several of the sites. Look for *Gemeinschaft* elements featured in the descriptions, as well as any *Gesellschaft* components that may be there. Write a report comparing the particular *Gesellschaft* emphases of the communities you explored. What factors in postindustrial societies may draw people to these features?

Chapter 5: How Sociologists Do Research

1. Use secondary analysis of census data to construct a table. Go to the 1990 Census Lookup page (http://www.census.gov/cdrom/lookup). Select the database, STF#c--Part 1. At the Retrieval Area page, click on the Submit bar. At the Data Retrieval Option page, click on the Submit bar. At the page headed, "Select the tables you wish to retrieve," page down to P70--Sex and Employment Status and click on the circle in front of the entry. Then go to the top of the page and click on the Submit bar. You should be presented with a table showing employment status of males and females. Depending on your WEB browser, you can either save the table or print it. (Netscape will allow both.) Use this data to practice constructing a table, as described in the table, "How to Read a Table."

Chapter 6: Societies to Social Networks

1. The importance of family as a primary group is emphasized by the contemporary catchwords "family values." Explore views of the family by using AltaVista (http://www.altavista.digital.com) with the search words, "family values." Read the arguments, commentaries, and offers of service, noting the aspects of primary groups addressed. Why are we so concerned by problems with families? Be ready to share your analysis with the class.

2. Are "electronic communities" really groups? Go to the Yahoo Usenet list (http://www.yahoo.com/News/ Usenet) and select Newsgroup Listing. At the listing, choose Anchorman, then alt. Read several of the exchanges in these news groups. Which of them seem to have group properties? Write a report discussing and defending your conclusions.

Chapter 7: Bureaucracy and Formal Organizations

1. The U. S. government bureaucracy is one of the largest and most complex in the world. Explore a small portion of its organization by accessing the Secretary of Defense's WEB page. Go to http://www.dtic.dla.mil/ defenselink and select Office of the Secretary. On the Secretary's page select The Organization Chart. Browse through the chart, looking for elements that are bureaucratic. What are the advantages of these bureaucratic features? What are the drawbacks? Can you think of any alternative ways of organizing the Department of Defense? Print the chart and bring it to class for discussion.

2. Women business owners are no longer rare in the United States. Go to the Women Business Network (http://www.frsa.com/womenbiz) and browse the site. Look at the issues raised, problems noted, and suggested solutions. Are there special difficulties faced by women business owners that are not faced by men? Discuss.

Chapter 8: Deviance and Social Control

1. Investigate changes in the crime index for major cities. Go to the FBI's home page (http://www.fbi. gov) and page down to the Uniform Crime Reporting Program. At "Preliminary 199- Statistics," select Report. On the Report page, select Table 4-- OFFENSES KNOWN TO THE POLICE. (The table number may change.) Select Proceed to Table 4 at the top of the page. Save or print the table. Note the changes in index crimes from the previous year in the column, "Crime Index total," for several different-sized cities in various regions of the country. Are there patterns in the changes, or is each city unique? Why do you think this is?

2. All people labeled "deviant" are not criminals. Use AltaVista (http://www.altavista.digital.com) with the search words "mental illness homelessness." Look at the discussion and declarations at several sites. Why do you think there is a perceived link between mental illness and homelessness? Do the two together constitute a social problem? Why? What are some possible solutions? Why hasn't out society already solved the problem? How likely are we to solve it in the future? (This would make an excellent panel discussion or debate.)

Chapter 9: Social Stratification in Global Perspective

1. Measuring social stratification in the U. S. Go to the 1990 Census Lookup page (http://venus.census.gov/cdrom/lookup). Select the database, STF3c--Part 1. At the Retrieval Area page, click on the Submit bar. At the Data Retrieval Option page, click on the Submit bar. At the page headed, "Change the tables you wish to retrieve," page down to P19--Poverty Status in 1989 by Race and Age, and click on the circle in front of the entry. Then go to the top of the page and click on the Submit bar. You should be presented with a table showing poverty status of five racial categories. Depending on your WEB browser, you can either save the table or print it. (Netscape will allow both.) Next, you need to compute the percentages for those in poverty for each racial category. (Your instructor may ask you to do this for age groups as well.) Total those in "Income in 1989 above poverty level: White." Do the same for those in "Income in 1989 below poverty level: White." Add the two figures and divide the sum found in "Income in 1989 below poverty level: White" by the result. This is the percent of White people whose income was below the poverty level in 1989. Now repeat the process for the other four racial categories.

After you have the percentages, construct a table of the results.

2. Measuring social stratification in Latin America. Go to Lanic (http://lanic.utexas.edu). Under the Subject Directory, select Economy. Page down to "Macroeconomic Data Resources" and select Latin American and the Caribbean Economic Social Data. Next, select Social Indicators, and then select Selected Social Indicators. Print this table. Next, backup to the previous page and select Midyear Population. Print this table as well. Using the column, "Human Development Index" (a composite of national income, literacy, and life expectancy) from the "Selected Social Indicators" table, compare nations of various sizes (from the "Midyear Population" table). Is Latin America a single unit of industrializing or least-industrial nations? Does size make a difference? Focus on two countries with different Human Development Index scores and research differences between them that might help explain their levels of development.

Chapter 10: Social Class in Contemporary Society

1. After reading the Thinking Critically About Social Controversy box, "Children in Poverty," go to the National Center for Children in Poverty page (http://cpmcnet.columbia.edu/dept/nccp) and select Child Poverty News and Issues." Browse the current and back issues. How does the issue of children in poverty relate to social class? Reflect on the question from the Children in Poverty box in your text, "...what specific programs would you recommend?" Present your conclusions in a panel discussion for your sociology class.

2. Welfare reform is an issue that continues to raise impassioned emotions, especially in presidential election years. Use AltaVista (http://www.altavista. igital.com) with the search words "welfare reform" to browse several sites related to the topic. What issues are currently being raised? How do the stands being taken seem to relate to social class differences in the United States? Explain why you think this is true?

Chapter 11: Inequalities of Gender

1. You have read in your text about the increasingly recognized problem of sexual harassment, as well as about its changing legal definitions. One place where this problem is being recognized and addressed--if controversially-- is on college campuses. It is highly probable that your school has a formal policy on sexual harassment. Get a copy of the policy, then go to AltaVista (http://www.altavista.digital.com) and enter the search words "sexual harassment" (without the quotation marks) and click on Submit. A list of ten sites will be presented. You can get more sites by going to the bottom of the page and selecting "Next Ten Hits." Most of the sites will be university policy statements.

Go to several of them and either save or print them. Compare the statements with each other and with that of your own school. Write a paper pointing out what they have in common and how they differ. Indicate any elements that you think should be added to or removed from your college's policy.

   2. As you learned in this chapter's section, "The Changing Face of Politics," a number of countries have had women presidents or prime ministers. Of course, the United States is not one of them. In this project you will have the chance to ask United States Senators about this issue. Access the Internet home page of the United States Congress (http://www.senate.gov). Select "Directory of Senators (by Name)." Select each name that seems to be female, and jot down those who are. Then choose one from your list and go back to her site. First make sure she offers an e-mail address (usually at the bottom of the page). If she has an address, read her speeches, policy statements, addresses, and whatever else she offers that reflects her political position. Compose a letter reflecting what you have learned (if anything) about the senator's position on the status of women in our society, and ask for details about a particular point. At the end of your message, ask her whether we should and will have a woman president. Include your postal mailing address, since she will likely acknowledge by e-mail and reply to your message by land mail.

Chapter 12: Inequalities of Race and Ethnicity

   1. Throughout the text, you have been led step-by-step through Internet projects. Now you have a chance to design your own. You've read about four minority groups in the U.S.: African Americans, Latino Americans, Asian Americans, and Native Americans. Now explore the net to learn about one of these groups. Here is a start: Go to http://www.yahoo.com and click in the blank box beside the "search" button. Type one of the following:"African American," "Asian American," "Chicano/Latino American," or "Native American," and click on "Search." Select one of the groups and start surfing! For example, after your search for "Native American," click on "Society and Culture:Culture:Native American" and then on "History." You will find "First person histories of the NW coast," where you will discover fascinating narratives, great graphics (if your system supports them), and a lot of information. You decide where to go with this. Your instructor will help you decide what final form your discussion or report will take. One warning: You may get so caught up in chasing additional links that you forget the other four courses you're taking.

   2. In the Sociology and the New Technology box "Technology and the African-American Experience," you learned about the impact of mechanical cotton pickers on the employment of African Americans working in the cotton fields. Perhaps more importantly, you were introduced to *The Promised Land* by Nicholas Lemann, a leading U.S. writer on race, class and poverty. Lemann is a contributing editor for Harpers Monthly, so we want to access their home page. First, go to http://www.theAtlantic.com/atlantic, then page down to "search the Atlantic Monthly Web site." In the search form, type "Nicholas Lemann" (without the quotation marks). You should now see a list of topics. First select "biography" and read this brief introduction to the author. Now go back to the previous page (the list of topics). If you can't get there, start over with the home page and repeat the search. First, you should read the article, "The Origins of the Underclass," which relates to the migration dealt with in The Promised Land. (The article is in two parts, which are not indicated in your search results; you will have to select both entries under "The Origins of the Underclass" to find which is Part I.) After you have read both parts of the article, go back to the search results and find "The Unfinished War" (another two-part article). Read both parts of Lemann's treatise on the War on Poverty. Return to your search results and select "Philadelphia: Black Nationalism on Campus." See whether you agree that multiculturalism and assimilation are not incompatible. Now write a paper summarizing each of the articles, then integrate the ideas into a single statement. To do this you will have to draw your own conclusions about relationships among the ideas. (To create a briefer project, you may want to assign the articles to separate students or groups.)

Chapter 13: Inequalities of Age

1. Let's do some role playing. You have been reading about some of the consequences of growing old in highly industrial societies like the United States. Now I want you to become old yourself. First you need to invent yourself. You are over 65-years-old and living in the United States. Now you take over: Exact age? Gender? Marital status? Exact place where you live (including size of town)? Own your home? Savings? Income? Health? Close relatives (who, where)? Work or retired? Interests or hobbies? Before you start, read this chapter again and be realistic in choosing attributes. Now for your Internet excursion. Go to http://www.yahoo.com, and select "Culture and Society." On the new page select "Age Groups." You should now see the categories "Geriatrics and Aging" and "Seniors." Now start to browsing. Find what you need for the life you invented. If you are in bad health, you might need information on health care. If your spouse has Alzheimer, you might look for support groups. If you are in good health and have enough money, why don't you plan a dream excursion with a "seniors tour"?

2. You have read in this chapter about the controversy surrounding Social Security and have been introduced to groups lobbying for the special interests of the elderly. These topics touch only the surface of government's involvement with aging. This project will allow you to explore some of the federal government programs. The Administration on Aging is the Executive Branch's chief agency aimed at providing for the needs of the elderly. Go to the agency's home page (http://www.aoa.dhhs.gov) and select "About" at the bottom of the screen. Select "Fact Sheet" on the new screen. Learn what you can about the AoA by reading what is on the page. You may find the organization chart of the agency interesting. When you finish, go back to the "About" page. (If you get lost, just start over with the AoA home page and select "About" again.) Three other topics besides the "Fact Sheet" are available: "The Older American Act," "The Administration on Aging" and "The Aging Network." Follow some of the links under each of these headings.

Chapter 14: The Economy: Money and Work

1. Now that you have learned about capitalism and socialism, as well as the trend toward the convergence of the two, you are invited to explore further. The Internet is a popular place for proponents of each ideology to expound on their view. I'm going to ask you to do another search because quite often the discussions and even their sites have very short lives. Go to AltaVista (http://www.altavista.digital.com) and change the window reading "10 results per page" to read "40 results per page" by clicking on the arrow beside the box. Enter the search terms "capitalism" and "socialism." (Don't put in the quotation marks or the word "and.") Now browse through the results of your search, selecting a variety of sites. Read the material at several of the sites and take notes on issues, positions, and analyses you find. In preparing this assignment I found outlines of college courses, book advertisements, student papers, a University of Texas Islamic club's position on capitalism, and even an entire book (Socialism from Below). After you have gone through the first 40 sites, you can select "next 40 hits" at the bottom of the final screen to see more sites. When you finish with your research, write a paper defining capitalism and socialism, and analyzing the positions adopted at various sites.

2. Work is one of the fundamental identities in industrial societies. Among the most devastating events that can happen to a worker is to become unemployed. You found some of the characteristics of unemployed people in the Perspectives box, "Who Is Unemployed."

Now let's look at regional unemployment in the United States, and introduce you to the data at the Bureau of Labor Statistics. Go to the BLS Home Page (http://stats.bls.gov) and select "Regional Information." Now select the region of the United States where you live. On the new screen, select "Most Requested Series." You should now see a list of topics with small squares in front of them. Click on each of the following:

- Unemployment Rate US, seasonally adjusted,
- Unemployment Rate (for your state),
- Unemployment Rate (for each state in the region adjacent to your state).

Go the bottom of the list. In the box labeled, "Years to search for," make sure the current year is highlighted. If it isn't, click on it. Now select "Retrieve Data." You should see tables for each of the categories you selected. Save or print these if you can; otherwise you will have to work from the screen. Note the rates for January and June for the United States and each state you selected. You are ready to construct a table with the data. Refer back to Table 5.1 in Chapter Five to refresh your memory on making tables. Now write a brief analysis of your table, and add your own ideas about why differences exist.

Chapter 15: Politics: Power and Authority

1. As you have learned, European democracies look somewhat different from that of the United States The parliamentary system of proportional representation does not provide for a distinct separation of power between the legislative and executive areas. Also unlike the United States, the political parties are noncentrist. Let's use the Internet to explore political parties in England. Go to the "British Politics Parties" site (http://www.agora.stm.it/politic/uk.htm). You should see a rather long list of parties in Great Britain, beginning with the Labour Party. Follow the links referring to parties in England. Explore each of the parties listed to discover as much as you can. Look for their history, philosophy, constituency and position on specific issues. How do they differ from United States parties? Write a paper comparing the parties on the basis of your findings.

2. You have read about the controversy surrounding lobbying, special-interest groups, and political action committees (PACs). Let's see what you can find out about them on the Internet. Go to Yahoo's list of sites under "Politics" (http://www.yahoo.com/Government/ Politics). Select "Interest Groups." You should now see three categories. "Lobbying Firms" points to firms advertizing their services. You might want to look at a few of these just to see what is being offered. The second category, "Political Action Committees," leads to several sites, most of them dealing with single issues at the state level (California's Ecovote Line, for example). If you are doing this project in an election year, you will find a fascinating CNN site that lists all of the contributions to major candidates (by state). It's interesting to see who supports whom, and for how much. The third category is "Public Interest Groups." Under this heading you will find several links to single issue groups: abortion issues, animal rights, etc. Look at several areas which you think are controversial or which particularly interest you. A report on this excursion will have to be very broad, so let's use a journal approach.

Chapter 16: The Family

1. As you have read in this chapter, you have learned that there are needs in every society that have to be met with some kind of family arrangements. These common cultural themes have been addressed in a variety of ways by societies throughout the world. Anthropologists have studied hundreds of these societies and have created concepts to refer to various kinship patterns. You have been introduced to a number of terms, such as *polygyny, exogamy, and matrilineal.* Now explore the fascinating world of kinship patterns by working through Brian Schwimmer's brief Internet tutorial, "Principles of Kinship." Access the site at http://www.umanitoba.ca/ anthropology/tutor. You

should see a list of topics, beginning with "Kin Fundamentals." Select this and follow it through. At the bottom of the page marked "Bilateral Kinship," select "Return to Main Menu," then select topic 2, "Systems of Descent." Go through all five areas, including the subtopics under 4, "Marriage Systems." Then look at the two ethnographic examples listed under 6: "A Turkish Peasant Village" and "Ancient Hebrews." Write an essay describing the kinship systems in the Turkish village and among the Hebrews, then analyze the United States system (as you have experienced it) using what you have learned in the tutorial.

2. You have read in this chapter about various kinds of family and kinship systems. There is a fascinating home page maintained by Heather Gidney, a student at LeMoyne College, that conducts the visitor through a virtual museum dedicated to the Iroquois, a matrilineal society. While the emphasis is not entirely on family arrangements, the visitor can see the impact of a female-based system of descent on many areas of life. Access the site (http://maple.lemoyne.edu/~gidneyhc/index.html). You should see the title, "Museum of Gender Studies of the Iroquois." Read the introduction below the map, then access "Matrilinear." After you go through the museum, write a paper comparing the Iroquois matrilineal system with that of the United States today.

3. You have been reading about various forms of abuse found in families. Suppose a friend came to you with a need for help in the matter of child abuse. You turn to your computer. Search the Web using AltaVista (http://www.altavista.digital.com) Enter the search terms "child abuse" (without the quotation marks) and select "Go get it." Browse for whatever information you can get. After looking at all of the pertinent sites on the Lycos results page, select "next 10 hits" at the bottom of the screen. When you finish researching the topic, write a paper in which you give as much useful information to your friend as you can.

Chapter 17: Education: Transferring Knowledge and Skills

1. As you read in the Sociology and the New Technology box, "Distance Learning: The Walls Come Tumbling Down," college courses are not restricted to the classroom anymore. One of the hottest topics on campuses today is "distance learning," involving everything from standard correspondence courses to the promise of truly interactive, multimedia instruction. This project gives you the opportunity to explore the cutting edge of this adventure in learning. Go to the Yahoo education site http://www.yahoo.com/ education Scroll down and select "On-Line Teaching and Learning." Browse through several of the sites listed to see the scope of what is offered. When you finish, go back to the "On-Line Teaching and Learning" site and select "Teaching and Learning on the World Wide Web." Fill in the search form with "distance education" (without the quotation marks) and click on "Go." When you get the results of your search, select "Globewide Network Academy." Then select "Online distance education course and catalog." Next select "View course by topic." Now you can explore the great number of courses available. You will be surprised at the number and variety of colleges offering instruction on the Internet. In fact, your college may be listed there. As you browse through the Web sites and track down courses and schools that offer them, keep a journal of the steps of your journey and your impressions along the way. Bring those to class to share with your classmates.

2. As you have discovered from reading this chapter (and perhaps from your own experiences), education in the United States faces many problems and wide controversy. In this project you will be asked to evaluate the content of two sites dealing with educational reform. Go to the Center for Education Reform (http://edreform.com) and Effective Education (http://www.interlog.com/ ~klima/ed.html). Browse through the two sites and then write a critique of what they have to offer. Are the problems they specify general or specific? Are they important? Are the solutions aimed at general reform or at reaching the goals of special interests? How would the problems raised be analyzed by functionalist, conflict, and symbolic interaction theory?

Chapter 18: Religion: Establishing Meaning

1. You were introduced to a brief survey of world religions in this chapter. You can explore most of these further through the Internet. Go to the Yahoo religion site (http://www.yahoo.com/society_and_culture/ religion). You should find links to sites dedicated to Buddhism, Christianity, Hinduism, Islam, and Judaism. You might like to browse a bit through some of these. When you finish, select one religion (not your own) and follow the links to as many sites as you can. As you go, take notes on history, beliefs, symbols, rituals, and organization. Use the information you gather to write a paper on the culture and social structure of the religion.

2. As you have discovered, sociologists use the terms *cult* and *sect* rather differently than they are often used in the media or in everyday conversation. As you start this project, write sociological definitions of church and sect. Now go to the Yahoo home page (http://www. yahoo.com) and use the search box by entering "cyberspace religions." You will see a number of links. (There were about twenty when the project was created.) Go through each of them and determine which are meant to be taken seriously. Of those, how many are representative of churches? On the remainder, use the definitions you created at the beginning of the project to determine what characteristics would indicate they are more sect-like or cult-like. Write a brief analysis of your findings and compare them with the conclusions of other students in the class.

Chapter 19: Medicine: Health and Illness

1. There is little doubt that the most alarming global threat from a single disease comes from AIDS. You should have gained some insight into its origin and scope as you read this chapter, but the amount of information possible in a brief account barely touches the scope of the topic. This project will give you the opportunity to explore AIDS in much greater depths. Access CDC/AIDS (gopher://gopher.niaid.nih.gov:70). Select "AIDS Related Information" and browse through several subdirectories. You might begin with the press releases and CDC Daily Summaries. Follow the links to find out as much as you can. When you have gathered enough information, write a paper on AIDS as a global threat.

2. In the Perspectives box, "Health Care in Three Worlds of Development," you encountered four examples of how the degree of industrialization is related to the level of health care. Look again at Table 19.6. Note that two indicators of health care are life expectancy at birth and infant mortality. In this project you will use these variables to test the hypothesis that the greater a nation's industrial development, the poorer its health care. First, go back to the two-page map of global stratification in chapter nine. Pick out ten countries in each of the categories "highly industrialized nations," "industrializing nations," and "least industrialized nations." Make a worksheet with these 30 countries in the left hand margin and two columns across the top, labeled Life Expectancy and Infant Mortality. Now access the CIA home page (http://www.odci.gov/cia/publications/pubs.html) and click on the book icon, "1995 World Factbook." You should see the alphabet running across the bottom of the screen. Now pick a nation from your list and select its initial. (For example, select J if you want Japan.) Now select the name of the country. Page down to the "People" section and look for your two variables, life expectancy and infant mortality. Write these values on your worksheet and go on to the next country on your list. When you have collected all of the data, create a table showing the values of the variables for each level of industrialization. Using the mean, average the rates for each category. Now write a report setting out your hypothesis, briefly explaining your methodology, and discussing your findings.

Chapter 20: Population and Urbanization

1. Sometimes studying demography can seem very abstract. Even when the implications for poverty and starvation are dealt with, the problems may appear very far from the relative safety of your own life. In this project you will be bringing the study of population to your own world. First, go the United States Census Bureau's Population Division site (http://www.census. gov/ftp/pub/population/www). Select "1990 Census Data," then page down to "1990 Census Lookup." Select "STF3a (detailed geography)." On the new page, you should find "Retrieve the areas you've selected" *marked*. Click on "Go to level: state--place" to mark it instead. Now page down, select your home state, and click on the "Select" bar. When the next page comes up, scroll down to select your home town, and again click on the "Select" bar. On the new page, "Choose tables" should already be marked, so just click on "Select." Now you should see a heading telling you to "Select the tables you wish to receive." For now, mark "P1 Persons" and "P7 Sex (2)." Click on "Submit." There should already be a dot before "HTML Format," so just click on "Submit" again. You should now see the two tables you asked for. You can print or save them. Now that you know how to get the data, go back to the "Select the tables..." page. Select tables that will tell you about the social conditions of your town. Do you have a large minority population? What is the state of the housing? Explore so that you can write a report on what just knowing about demographic variations tells you about your home town.

2. Look again at the list of the world's largest cities in Table 20.2. Have you ever visited any of them? At most, you have probably been in only one or two. In this project you will have the opportunity to tour most of them by way of the Internet. As you access the sites, please remember that the sponsors include government, commercial agencies, and academic sources, so the emphases of the sites can vary widely. Tour as many cities as you can, then bring your impressions to class to share with other tourists. The sites: (Some addresses may be case sensitive, so copy each exactly.)

- Tokyo (http://www.metro.tokyo.jp/portrait/portrait.htm)
- Mexico City (http://www.remag.com/mexcity)
- Seoul (http://iworld.net/Korea/travel/f282.html)
- New York City (http://astor.mediabridge.com/ nyc)
- Bombay (http://www.bchs.uh.edu/~mdoshi/ Bombay/Bombay.html)
- Tehran (http://www.coe.uncc.edu/~fsheikhb/ tehranhistory.html)
- Cairo (http://pharos.bu.edu/Egypt/Cairo)
- Calcutta (http://www.city.net/countries/india/ calcutta)
- Moscow (http://sunsite.unc.edu/sergei/Exs/ Moscow/moscow.html)

Chapter 21: Collective Behavior and Social Movements

1. As you discovered in reading this chapter, riots are a form of collective behavior. The nation's most destructive riot up to the time this book was being written was in Los Angeles in 1992. Because of the coverage it received, the event can be analyzed using secondary sources. Access the Hubert H. Humphrey Institute of Public Affairs http://www.hhh.umn.edu/ PUBPOL/PUBPOL-D/9505/0032.html) You should now be in the Institute's "Listserve Archives." The topic heading should read "Re: LA Riot: Q0) Conference instructions." When you have read the page, click on "Thread." As you travel through the discussion, watch for "next in thread" and "in reply to." Follow these as you study the exchange. In your research, take notes that will help you illustrate the theories of collective behavior you have read about. For Blumer's theory, can you find evidence of general social unrest preceding the riot? What was the "exiting event"? Is there evidence of crowd milling? Can you find a common object of attention and common crowd impulses?

Richard Burke sees collective behavior as calculated, rational action. Is there evidence of people balancing the rewards and costs of becoming involved? Now consider emergent norm theory. First, can you find any evidence of participants having different motives for their involvement, or is everyone simply angry over the precipitating event? Are these related to the rise of crowd norms not appropriate to everyday behavior? Write a paper applying the theories to the riot as it is reflected in the exchanges found in the Archive.

2. You have learned about four types of social movements, each having a different kind of goal. Look at an example of each kind and note the elements that seem to be characteristic. Alternative social movements try to change people's behavior in some way, such as quitting smoking (Tobacco BBS: http://www.tobacco. org). Redemptive movements stress religious conversion (Origins of the Pentecostal Movement: http://www.oru. edu/library/holyspirit/pentorg1.html). Reformative movements attempt to change aspects of society (Environment: http://www.greenpeace.org), while transformative movements want to change the entire social order (Rastifarians: http://www.cwrl.utexas.edu/ ~bill/e309m/students/marley/history/rastafar/index. html). Write a paper comparing the four movements in terms of goals, memberships, sympathetic publics outside the movement, and relationships with authorities. Is there evidence of how each movement has attempted to mold public opinion? Why do you think each of the social movements has had whatever success it has gained?

Chapter 22: Social Change, Technology, and the Environment

1. Rapid technological change raises new issues for public debate and new areas for sociologists to study. The Center for Democracy and Technology (http://www.cdt.org/index.html) is an example of a "watchdog" group presenting a point of view on the impact of technological policy decisions and related issues on United States society. Read one or more of the headline articles from their site. In a one- or two-page paper, answer the following questions: What issues are of concern? What seems to be the viewpoint of those at CDT? What might be the opposing arguments to this view?

2. This chapter's summary of the impact of social change on the environment in highly industrial nations suggests that the "bottom line" involves a decision for the global growth machine or the earth. Attempts at balancing these concerns, especially among the least industrialized nations, are referred to as "sustainable environment." Read the section, "Social Change and the Natural Environment," then look at a collection of efforts at creating sustainable environments by accessing Solstice (http://solstice.crest.org). Read the information on Solstice itself, then click on the "Related net sites" to see a large and varied list of sites dedicated to environmental concerns. Browse several of them. Is the sustainable environment theme aimed only at least industrial nations or is it global? What are some policies and practices that you think might work with nations at different levels of industrialization? Are there any that would be practical in nearly all countries? How likely is it that any of the policies will be adopted by the United States? What do you think the future holds: growth machine or the earth? Or a compromise enabling a sustainable environment?

Henslin's Essentials of Sociology

Chapter 1: The Sociological Perspective

As you discovered when you read the section in your text, "The Dilemma of Values in Social Research," maintaining objectivity is a great challenge to researchers. This is especially true when sociologists are faced with comparing vastly different segments of a society with many patterns of living. It is equally true when they study widely divergent societies, as anthropologists have discovered in the last 100 years. To examine a variety of peoples and to see whether you can maintain your own objectivity, go to the "NativeWeb Home Page," (http://www.maxwell. syr.edu/nativeweb). When you arrive, page down until you see ||**subject**||**geographic regions**||**nations/ peoples**|| (and so on). Click on geographic regions. You will see a list of areas on the new page. Browse through a number of societies. What do most of them have in common? What are the most diverse elements? Now decide on four rather different peoples and take notes for a 3-4 page paper covering the following questions: 1) Which elements of the societies are you comfortable with? 2) Which ones make you most uncomfortable? 3) How objective do you think you could be doing a field study in each of the four? 4) Briefly describe as objectively as possible what you see as the most important elements in each.

Chapter 2: Culture

One of the fascinating aspects of studying about culture lies in the concept of subculture. As you have probably learned from reading this chapter in your text, subcultures are groups with norms, roles, and lifestyles which deviate extensively from those in their society's general culture. What the project entails is your looking at the characteristics of some religious groups to see if they seem to be subcultures rather than just dominant-cultural groups. (You need to remember that religious groups which are based on another society's religion are often a subculture.) The project you are about to work on will lead you into the particular realm of religious subcultures. To begin, direct your computer to Mike's Religion Page (http://www.servtech.com/public/mcroghan/religion.htm). Page down into the "Table of Faiths," and find "Buddhism." Look in the right-hand column ("Sects"), and click on "Soka-Gakkai." On the new page, click on several of the listed subjects and read the material, looking for information on the degree to which their beliefs and behaviors deviate from the dominant culture in the U.S. When you finish you should be able to make a good guess as to whether Soka Gakkai is a subculture in this country. Finally, go back to the "Table of Faiths" page and choose three nonBuddhist religions. Jot these down, then click on each of your choices to find a specific religious group. Follow the procedure you used in studying Soka Gakkai. When you have completed your research, write a paper of 3-5 pages comparing the groups as possible subcultures.

Chapter 3: Socialization

In this project you will be critiquing a graduate student's paper on sociobiology, a controversial theory that looks at biological factors as almost completely determining human social behavior. In this chapter you have read a little bit about the nature-nurture controversy--whether biology or society is the main socializer of human behavior. Applying what you have learned and using your critical-thinking skills, you should be able to make some general arguments about the paper you read, even though you know little or nothing about sociobiology itself. Go to Steve Mizrach's critique of sociobiology (http://www.clas.ufl.edu/anthro/scholarly/bio-creative.html). Because it is written in an understandable way, you should be able to comprehend it. After you have read the article, address each of the following questions in a short paper: 1) What is your general impression of the validity of Mizrach's paper? (Does it "ring true"?) Why? 2) How well does the sociobiological theory of genius and madness explain them? What do they fail to explain? 3)

Is Mizrach fair to sociobiology in his conclusions? Bring your paper to class. Your instructor may want the class to exchange papers or form small groups to share their ideas.

Chapter 4: Social Structure and Social Interaction

In this chapter you learned about the statuses and roles found in groups. Although the topic of formal organization is explored in the next chapter, you will be looking at the organization charts of large organizations to see what the positions (statuses) are and how they differ from group to group. Point your computer to Yahoo's Page (http://www.yahoo.com) and enter the search terms "organization chart" (without the quotation marks). Go to the bottom of the page and click on the AltaVista bar. On the new page you will see the first ten of hundreds of sites containing organization charts. Your task is to describe and compare statuses. Start by clicking on two or three sites and note the similarities of the positions revealed. Are there any major differences? Once you get a feel for the charts, select several sites in each of two organizational types. For example, you might look at organizations for military, government, education, or religion. Take notes on the general similarities of statuses between organizational types, and differences that seem to indicate the type of organization. Select a third site involving another type of organization and add similar notes concerning it. (Also get an organization chart from your college or university if it is available.) Write a two or three page paper on your findings.

Chapter 5: Social Groups in a Socially Diverse Society

In Chapter Five, you are introduced to George Ritzer's concept of "The McDonaldization of society," which involves the rationalization of the routine tasks of everyday life. Read the Down-to-Earth Sociology box on page 108, then write a paragraph describing the general process. Go to the McDonaldization Home page

(http://www.wam.umd.edu/~allan/mcdonald.html).
Read the page, then click on the italicized word
"*rationalization.*" After reading the new page, go back
to the McDonaldization Home site and click on
"Efficiency," "Calculability," "Predictability," and
"Control," and read each page. Next, click on the
"frontiers of McDonaldization" at the bottom of the
first screen and check out the Max Headroom episode.
Finally click on "irrationality of rationality" on the
second screen, and read the page. (If you are hooked,
click on the Dilbert button and see if you can find any
cartoons involving the irrationality of rationality in the
work place.) After you have finished your research,
write a two-part paper. In part one, discuss the general
idea of McDonaldization and its specific elements. In
the second part of the paper, apply the concept to some
aspect of your college or university, and discuss the
degree to which each of the McDonaldization concepts
you learned from your Web research applies to the
situation.

Chapter 6: Deviance and Social Control

As you have discovered in reading this chapter,
criminal behavior is only one part of deviance. Still, it
is an important part. In this project, you have the
opportunity to do extensive research on a topic of your
own choosing and write either a short or lengthy paper,
depending on your instructor's preferences. Go to Cecil
Greek's Criminal Justice home page (http://www.fsu.
edu/~crimdo/cj.htm) and browse through the topics
offered. (This is probably the most complete CJ site on
the Internet.) You should now be able to form a
research question. Proceed following links relating to
your topic, taking notes as if you were working in a
library. When you finish, write your paper. (Don't
forget a good paper has an introduction and a
conclusion, and is well organized into topical sections
and paragraphs.)

Chapter 7: Social Stratification in Global Perspective

Is there a social stratification among the nations of the world? If we classify countries as highly industrialized, industrializing, and least industrialized, we should be able to find variables which will indicate levels of stratification among the levels. In this project you will be comparing an industrializing nation (Indonesia) with a highly industrialized one (the U.S.). In order to do this you will be using two sources, the Internet and the library. First go to the BPS Web site (http://www.bps. go.id/socwel/swtables.html) where you will find a list of social welfare indicators. Either click on each one or just page down to look at the tables. (If you can, it would be a good idea to print the entire page.) Now go to the library and get the latest Statistical Abstract of the U.S. Find as many comparisons with Indonesia as you can. Look in the index at such topis as immunization, education, crime, etc. You should find enough comparisons to make some rough comparisons of several variables. After you have completed your research, write a brief report of analysis and interpretation: What are some of the marked differences between the two nations? Are any of them surprising? What might be some of the social forces contributing to the levels of social welfare in each of the two countries?

Chapter 8: Social Class in Contemporary Society

As you begin this project, read the section of Chapter Eight entitled "Wealth" (pages 172-175). Does the extreme difference between the rich and the poor surprise you? The disparities become clearer as you look at more detailed data. With this in mind, go to "How the pie is sliced" (http://epn.org/prospect/22/22wolf.html) and read Wolff's article. (You may want to print it out so you can make notes on the copy.) Write a one or two page paper summarizing the content of the article, addressing the following questions: 1) Of all of the growth in wealth and income in the 1980s, how much was gained by the richest 1%? By the bottom 80%? 2)What is the long term trend in the distribution of wealth and income? 3) How does the level of inequalities in the U.S. compare with other industrialized nations? In the final two sections of your paper, discuss why the rich gained so much in the 1980s, and the possible solutions to the problem of extreme inequalities.

Chapter 9: Inequalities of Race and Ethnicity

In order to have a context for understanding what the inequalities of race and ethnicity mean to group members, it would be good to use a method employed by anthropologists. In doing participant observation, their first step is to immerse themselves in the culture they are going to study. Go to Gravity (http://www.newsavanna.com/gravity/gb.acgi$azone.21zz21), a WEB site that provides the opportunity for African Americans to chat with each other. Unless you are part of it, you are usually not able to get in on conversations within any group. By reading the exchanges you can watch for evidence on how inequality affects a group. Return to the site once a day for several days to check on current exchanges. If you are African American, compare the attitudes expressed with your own experiences. You might even join the chat and exchange ideas with others. Click on the button beside "list all topics." You should find a long list of topics. Choose one that seems to be related to feeling or experiences of inequality and read the exchanges. Do this with several topics, making notes from the pertinent comments. Now write a brief paper answering three questions: 1) Is the exchange similar to what you think and talk about? If not, how does it differ? 2) What kinds of experiences do you think lie behind the discussion? 3) Are discussion styles and topics similar to what you would expect within other Internet groups, such as a site dedicated to child abuse or one on fly fishing? Take both your paper and your notes to class where you will meet in a discussion with other students to exchange ideas. (Instructor: It would be good to include people from different racial or ethnic groups in as many of the discussion groups as possible.)

Chapter 10: Inequalities of Gender and Age

As you read the section in this chapter on "Gender and violence," note that there are several types of violence involving men and women. It should come as no surprise that overwhelmingly men are the aggressors and women the victims. As a college student, it should be of great concern to you that the most frequent type of gender-related crimes is rape, and that it is increasingly recognized that date rape is a the fastest growing area of these crimes. To look at date rape, we need to look at the more general category of acquaintance rape. Go to the "Sexual Assault Information Page" (http://www.cs. utk.edu/~bartley/saInfoPage.html). Click on "Acquaintance Rape" and you should see a list of 10 or 12 links to sites having information or other resources. Gather information from six of these sites:
1) Acquaintance Rape (the first listing, not the second); Connecticut Sexual Assault Crisis Services; "Friends" Raping Friends; Myths and Facts about Acquaintance Rape; and Sexual Assault and Rape: Advice to Men. When you finish with your research, you should be able to write a short paper on the incidence, characteristics, and prevention of date rape, as well as on some resources for women who are victims. If you want to gather more information, follow the links given at the various sites you visit.

Chapter 11: Politics and the Economy: Leadership and Work in the Global Village

In this chapter, Henslin talks about three eras in the history of economic systems: preindustrial, industrial, and postindustrial. Perhaps the most crucial for all of us is the one we are living in, "Postindustrial Societies: The Information Age." First, read the entire section on "The transformation of economic systems," paying special attention to the nature of postindustrial society. Next, go to the Web page of "The Millennial Files" (http://www.mmmfiles.com) and read the entire article.

(You might want to print each section so it is easier to take notes.) When you finish, write a five or six page paper on the background, characteristics, problems, and future of postindustrial society.

Chapter 12: Marriage and the Family: Our Introduction to Society

When sociologists look at the problems faced by families, they usually include the special difficulties faced by children, often in a global perspective. This project will involve your participating in a panel reporting on the state of the world's children and introduce you to the world's largest organization devoted to them, the United Nations agency UNICEF. Go to their home page (http://www.unicef.org) and page down to "Organization," and click on "About UNICEF." Read about the agency to give yourself some background on its purpose, goals, and activities. Return to the UNICEF Home Page and click on "The State of the World's Children," an annual report published by UNICEF. On the new page, click on "Summary." Note the important issues and the most crucial problems facing children throughout the world. Go back to "The State of the World's Children" page and click on fact sheets. If you do not have an Acrobat reader, you will have to download a copy. Click on "download the reader" and follow the instructions for installing it on your machine. Back at the Report page, click on "Fact Sheets," and click on the "Download fact sheets as a PDF." (Because servers change aspects of their sites from time to time, you may find that UNICIF no longer uses the Acrobat (PDF) reader, but instructions will be given on how to use the reader currently employed.) Now go back to the Report page and click on "Download the PDF version" to get the entire report. It will be your main source of information. This seems like a great deal of reading material, but in forming a panel group, each of you can focus on a different aspect of the report. (Everyone should read all of the other materials described above.)

Chapter 13: Education and Religion: Cross-Generational Transfer of Knowledge, Skills and Meaning

This chapter focuses primarily on the theories of education. The project will allow you to analyze data on which these theories are based. Go to the National Center for Educational Statistics site (http://www.ed.gov/NCES) and click on "Publications." On the new page click on "General Publications." On the general publications page, move down near the bottom and click on "Mini-Digest of Educational Statistics: (date)" where you should see a chart labeled "The Mini-Digest of Education Statistics: (date)" and an extensive list of data locations. Under "Educational Outcomes," click on "Dropouts" and print or download the figure and table you find there. Note the trends between 1970 and the present in Figure 7. Does this suggest anything to you about educational inequalities? Look at the details in Table 16. Are the trends constant through the years or do they fluctuate greatly from year to year? Next, back up to the previous screen ("Mini-Digest...."), look under "Elementary and Secondary Schools," click on "Enrollment by Race and Ethnicity." and print or download Table 6. The table shows the percentage of children in school for three racial or ethnic groups. What can you conclude from the table? Look at the distribution as functionalists, conflict theorists, and symbolic interactionists might. (You might need to read again the sections in the first half of this chapter.) How would each explain the patterns revealed in the table? To continue the project, browse among other topics on the Mini-Digest page. Look for evidence of educational inequalities involving race, gender, or other meaningful variables you might discover. On the basis of your research, write a paper on educational inequalities and attempt to interpret each of the patterns you found by using the three theories you encountered earlier.

Chapter 14: Population and Urbanization

This project centers on the topic of world hunger. Read the section in your text entitled, "A planet with no space for the good life?" and take special note of "Why are people starving?". What are the main arguments of the Malthusian and anti-Malthusian theories of world hunger? If the main problem is distribution of food and not its production, which of the two seems more nearly correct? In looking at information on the Internet, you will be comparing two sites dedicated to research on and the elimination of starvation around the world. Go to "The 30 Hour Famine" page (http://www. 30hourfamine.org/whats.html" and browse the site. Then go to "The HungerWeb" (http://www.brown.edu/ Departments/World_Hunger_Program) and read through the page. When you have finished, go back to the top of the page and click on "Alan Shawn Feinstein World Hunger Program" (overview). Follow the links by clicking on items in the list. Write a brief paper in which you include both the theories and patterns of world hunger. Elaborate on the efforts to solve the problem.

Chapter 15: Social Change: Technology, Social Movements, and the Environment

Read the section, "Social Movements as a Source of Social Change." You will be using this information to analyze several social movements having Web pages. Go to Calyx's Activist Groups (http://www.calyx.net/ activist.html) and investigate several of the groups listed. For each group, try to determine if it has the characteristics of a social movement, what type of movement it is, and whether or not you think it will be successful. While you probably have your own ideas about what will or will not work, base your discussion on the text section, "On the success and failure of social movements." Compare your findings with others in your class.

INDEX

NOTES

Use this space for additional addresses as you explore the WWW...

Title:
Description:
Address:

Title:
Description:
Address:

Title:
Description:
Address:

Title:
Description:
Address:

Title:
Description:
Address:

Title:
Description:
Address:

Title:
Description:
Address:

Title:
Description:
Address:

NOTES

Use this space for additional addresses as you explore the WWW...

Title:
Description:
Address:

Title:
Description:
Address:

Title:
Description:
Address:

Title:
Description:
Address:

Title:
Description:
Address:

Title:
Description:
Address:

Title:
Description:
Address:

Title:
Description:
Address:

NOTES

Use this space for additional addresses as you explore the WWW...

Title:
Description:
Address:

Title:
Description:
Address:

Title:
Description:
Address:

Title:
Description:
Address:

Title:
Description:
Address:

Title:
Description:
Address:

Title:
Description:
Address:

Title:
Description:
Address:

NOTES

Use this space for additional addresses as you explore the WWW...

Title:
Description:
Address:

Title:
Description:
Address:

Title:
Description:
Address:

Title:
Description:
Address:

Title:
Description:
Address:

Title:
Description:
Address:

Title:
Description:
Address:

Title:
Description:
Address:

NOTES

Use this space for additional addresses as you explore the WWW...

Title:
Description:
Address:

Title:
Description:
Address:

Title:
Description:
Address:

Title:
Description:
Address:

Title:
Description:
Address:

Title:
Description:
Address:

Title:
Description:
Address:

Title:
Description:
Address:

NOTES

Use this space for additional addresses as you explore the WWW...

Title:
Description:
Address:

Title:
Description:
Address:

Title:
Description:
Address:

Title:
Description:
Address:

Title:
Description:
Address:

Title:
Description:
Address:

Title:
Description:
Address:

Title:
Description:
Address:

NOTES

Use this space for additional addresses as you explore the WWW...

Title:
Description:
Address:

Title:
Description:
Address:

Title:
Description:
Address:

Title:
Description:
Address:

Title:
Description:
Address:

Title:
Description:
Address:

Title:
Description:
Address:

Title:
Description:
Address:

NOTES

Use this space for additional addresses as you explore the WWW...

Title:
Description:
Address:

Title:
Description:
Address:

Title:
Description:
Address:

Title:
Description:
Address:

Title:
Description:
Address:

Title:
Description:
Address:

Title:
Description:
Address:

Title:
Description:
Address:

NOTES

Use this space for additional addresses as you explore the WWW...

Title:
Description:
Address:

Title:
Description:
Address:

Title:
Description:
Address:

Title:
Description:
Address:

Title:
Description:
Address:

Title:
Description:
Address:

Title:
Description:
Address:

Title:
Description:
Address: